really simple english grammar

essentials

carolyn humphries

foulsham

LONDON • NEW YORK • TORONTO • SYDNEY

foulsham

The Publishing House, Bennetts Close, Cippenham,
Slough, Berkshire, SL1 5AP, England

ISBN 0-572-02811-3

Cover photograph © Eye Wire Collections

Printed in Great Britain by Cox & Wyman Ltd, Reading, Berkshire

Contents

Introduction

If you've ever tried to use a grammar book to look up something straightforward – such as when to use 'that' or 'which', or where to put the apostrophe when a word already ends in 's' – you'll know it's virtually impossible to find what you want. Even the books supposedly designed for people with no knowledge of grammar seem to use complicated jargon, and you need a natural ability for the subject and a desire to plough through endless paragraphs of complicated text just to pinpoint your problem. When it comes to spelling, dictionaries aren't much help either – if you can't spell a word, how are you supposed to find it in the first place?

This book is different. It's a concise and practical reference book, all about best practice in written communication. It contains everything you need to know to help you write clearly and correctly, but it won't confuse you with complicated terminology, unnecessary detail or convoluted explanations. Everything is in plain, sensible English with lots of examples illustrating each point. Most topics are cross-referenced to help you find them easily and, where necessary, information is placed in more than one section so wherever you look for it, you'll find it straight away.

Really Simple English Grammar is designed as a useful, working guide to help you avoid all the most common written mistakes – and to improve your spoken English at the same time. It is not designed as a formal reference to cover every conceivable grammatical point and it deliberately includes only the most common grammatical terms so you can really get to grips with the basics. Of course, if you do get hooked on grammar – you may not believe me but it can be fascinating! – you can go on to study it further.

Keep this reference book to hand, ready to dip into when you're writing anything from a letter to a literary masterpiece. You'll soon find that you can impress your friends and colleagues with your new-found expertise and you'll have much more confidence in the way you use English.

The hardest bit – where to start

Don't be put off when you glance at the first chapter. It looks complicated but it isn't. The problem with grammar is that there is no beginning and no end – it's more of a continuous circular route. For instance, it's hard to explain how to construct a sentence without first explaining what verbs and nouns are; but it's just as hard explaining what verbs and nouns are without first defining what constitutes a sentence!

This book starts with the basic parts of speech so that you can become familiar with what each word in a sentence does. Then I take you through how to build up your sentences, putting in the correct punctuation as you go; and finally the last chapters guide you through those little idiosyncrasies of English spelling that catch even the best of us out from time to time.

You don't have to start at the beginning and read the whole book like a novel. You may just want to dip into the section you need to check a particular point that is bothering you – there is a comprehensive index at the back to make it easy. But, if you do want to learn from scratch, you can start from Chapter 1 and gradually build up your knowledge, chapter by chapter.

You'll be amazed at how quickly you begin to understand English grammar and all its irregularities. Soon you'll find yourself noticing when other people make mistakes. But don't be a bore and point them all out – just enjoy being a silent, smug know-it-all!

Chapter 1
Parts of Speech

Everything we write and say is expressed in words, which may stand alone or be linked together into phrases and sentences. Under the rules of grammar, words are put into different categories called *parts of speech* and the first step towards using speaking and writing correctly is to learn what these are and how they function. In this chapter we are going to explain what the parts of speech are and how you use them. The parts of speech are:

Verbs	Words that involve being or doing	see page 9
Nouns	Words that name	see page 20
Pronouns	Words that replace nouns	see page 25
Adjectives	Words that describe	see page 31
Adverbs	Words that qualify or tell you more	see page 36
Prepositions	Words that link a noun or pronoun to the rest of the sentence	see page 38
Conjunctions	Words that join two parts of a sentence	see page 41

> ⚠ **Watch out for vowels and consonants**
> The English alphabet has five vowels: *a, e, i, o, u*. Each single vowel may be referred to as short or long, depending on the way it is pronounced.
>
> | | | | |
> |---|---|---|---|
> | Short a | h**a**t | Long a | h**ay** |
> | Short e | b**e**d | Long e | th**e**se |
> | Short i | s**i**t | Long i | r**i**de |
> | Short o | p**o**d | Long o | m**o**le |
> | Short u | b**u**t | Long u | fl**u**te, c**u**te |
>
> The remainder of the letters of the alphabet are consonants. The pronunciation of each is constant, with the exception of *c* and *g*, which may be either hard or soft.
>
> | | | | |
> |---|---|---|---|
> | Hard c | **c**at, pani**c**, rac**c**oon | Soft c | fa**c**e, **c**ereal |
> | Hard g | **g**o, ba**g** | Soft g | **g**iraffe, ra**g**e |

In written English, these parts of speech are strung together into groups of words, to form *sentences*. Each sentence can be broken down into short sections, called *clauses* and *phrases*. In order to write correctly, you must understand the meaning of these terms.

Sentence A complete statement, including a verb, that can stand on its own.

Clause A complete statement, including a verb, that is part of a longer sentence.

Phrase A group of words, without a verb, that is part of a longer sentence.

Paragraph A group of sentences on the same topic.

⚠ **Watch out for syllables**

A syllable is simply a single sound in a word. *Cat* has one syllable. *Hedgehog* has two syllables. *Kangaroo* has three syllables.

Verbs

Verbs used to be known as 'doing' or 'action' words. Some verbs clearly involve activity, for example

> to run

> to grab

However, this definition is misleading because some verbs may involve no apparent action at all, such as

> to be

> to think

> to thunder

It is perhaps better to think of verbs as 'function' words.

There are several forms of each verb. The form of the verb given here, where it is preceded by *to* – as in *to be, to go, to sing* – is known as the *infinitive*.

⚠ Watch out for split infinitives

The famous line from the TV show *Star Trek* – 'to boldly go where no man has gone before' – is a classic example of a split infinitive. This is when an adverb (here, *boldly*) is placed between the words of the infinitive (*to go*). This used to be considered a heinous grammatical crime but today we are not so fussy; in fact, you can use it for emphasis, as Captain Kirk does here! It is no bad thing, however, to be aware when you are splitting an infinitive – in case you are challenged by a traditionalist – and you should always make sure it doesn't alter the sense or make the sentence awkward.

By definition, **all sentences must contain a verb.** If there is no verb, it's not a sentence!

There are two types of verb. Some verbs need a word known as an *object* in order to make sense – these are the verbs where you are doing something to something or with something. They are known as *transitive* verbs.

> I beat the drum.
> He stroked the cat.

Some verbs don't need an object in order to make sense; the function they describe can stand alone. These are *intransitive* verbs.

> I cried.
>
> They rejoiced.

Tenses

The tense of a verb shows when it takes place – in the present, past or future.

Present tense

The present tense is used when things are happening **now**.

> The guard stands in front of the palace.
>
> I love my dog.
>
> We want an apology.

In some instances, you can use a form of present tense to show that something is happening now and is continuing to happen. This uses *am, are* or *is* plus the *present participle,* which is simply the infinitive form of the verb with *-ing* added on.

> The guard is standing in front of the palace.
>
> You are walking to the shop.

Native English speakers do not have any trouble deciding which form of the present tense to use but this is an endless source of difficulty to foreigners.

> We are wanting a map of London.   ✗
>
> We want a map of London.   ✓

For the rules on how to add the *-ing* to verbs, see Forming Present and Past Participles on page 19.

Present participles as nouns: Words ending in *-ing* are often used on their own as nouns. If you need to know whether a word ending in *-ing* is a present participle of a verb or a noun, look at what it does in the sentence.

In this example, *dancing* is a present participle of the verb *am dancing*.

> When I am dancing, I am very light on my feet.

In the next example, *dancing* is a noun; the verb is *is*.

> Dancing is very good exercise.

⚠ **Watch out for sentences that start with a present participle**

If you start a sentence with a present participle, you must remember that it relates to the person doing the main action in the sentence. Look at these two examples.

> The steak is very good here. Having said that, the fish is
> good too.   ✗

This is wrong. It sounds as though the fish is recommending the steak!

> I know the steak is really good here. Having said that,
> I can recommend the fish as well.   ✓

This is correct. The person speaking is making the recommendations.

Past tense

The past tense is used when the action or function has already happened and is now over.

> I considered the problem.
>
> You ran home.
>
> She liked the dress.
>
> We selected the words.
>
> They were sad.

There is a second form of past tense, which uses *has* or *have* plus the *past participle* to show when something has been completed. The past participle is formed by adding *-d* or *-ed* to the infinitive form of verb, like the past tense, but some end in *-n* or *-en* and some do not change at all. The list on page 17 gives common examples but there are no easy rules so you will have to use a dictionary if you aren't sure.

> We have informed the police.
>
> They have completed the task.
>
> I have eaten my meal.
>
> You have tried my patience.
>
> He has lived in the house for 20 years.

For the rules on how to add *-d* or *-ed* to verbs, see Forming Present and Past Participles on page 19.

Past participles can also be used as adjectives (see page 35).

> ⚠ **Watch out for *providing* and *provided***
> If something has to happen before something else can happen, then use the past participle, not the present.
>
> *Providing the rain stops, the children can ride their bikes.* ✗
>
> This first example is wrong. It sounds as though the children are providing the rain stops. You should say:
>
> *Provided the rain stops, the children can ride their bikes.* ✓

The subjunctive: This is a form of verb that is now almost obsolete in English. However, you will have heard it in expressions such as 'If I were you'. It is used when something is imagined, when you know you are not dealing with facts. It is also used when you wish for something but it can't really happen.

I wish I were a millionaire.

You can also rearrange the order of the words in the sentence and use *were I* instead of *if I were*.

Were I to win the lottery, I would buy a mansion.

Because the subjunctive is so rare nowadays, it is best avoided if you are in any doubt as to how to use it.

Future tense

The future tense is used when things are going to happen later, in the future. To form the future tense, *will* or *shall* is placed before the verb. It is grammatically correct to use *shall* with *I* and *we*, and *will* with *he, she, it, you* and *they*. However, in modern usage, *will* is more commonly used for all.

> He will mend the car next week.
> It will look better in the morning.
> They will go on holiday next summer.
> We shall meet again soon.

⚠ **Watch out for *shall* and *will* for emphasis**

The rule for using *shall* and *will* is reversed if you want to give more force to the words.

> I **will** pass my driving test.
> You **shall** go to the ball.

I'll and you'll: These are short for *I shall* and *you will* and are used in exactly the same way. Short forms like this, which are called *contractions,* are only used in spoken English and informal writing.

Shan't and won't: These are short for *shall not* and *will not* so they are the negative versions of 'shall' and 'will' and are used in exactly the same way. They are only used in spoken English and informal writing.

See also Apostrophes on page 53.

Conditional tense

This is formed by prefacing the verb with *should* or *would*. Conditional verbs imply that an action to be taken in the future depends on (i.e. is conditional on) something else. The choice of which to use follows the same rules as *shall* and *will*.

> I **should like** to buy a car if I pass my driving test.
>
> They **would like** to go out tomorrow but they must wait to see if it is fine.

The conditional tense can also be used to mean *ought to*. In this case, you use *should* with every pronoun.

> I should eat less.
>
> You should know what he said about you.

⚠ **Watch out for *should of* and *could of***

Many people say *should of* and *could of* when they mean *should have* and *could have*. This has crept into common usage through mispronunciation and is a bad mistake.

> I should of told him about the meeting.   ✗
>
> I should have told him about the meeting.   ✓

Regular and irregular verbs

In most cases, to change a verb to the past tense and the past participle, you add *-ed* or *-d* to the infinitive form of verb. Those that follow this rule are known as *regular* verbs. For the rules on forming the past participles of regular verbs, see page 19.

Regular verbs

Infinitive	Past tense	Past participle
to look	(I) looked	(I have) looked
to love	(I) loved	(I have) loved

A few verbs can take -t or -ed in the past tense; both are correct.

Infinitive	Past tense	Past participle
to burn	(I) burned /burnt	(I have) burned/burnt
to dream	(I) dreamed/dreamt	(I have) dreamed/dreamt
to dwell	(I) dwelled/dwelt	(I have) dwelled/dwelt
to lean	(I) leaned/leant	(I have) leaned/leant
to leap	(I) leaped/leapt	(I have) leaped/leapt
to learn	(I) learned/learnt	(I have) learned/learnt
to smell	(I) smelled/smelt	(I have) smelled/smelt
to spell	(I) spelled/spelt	(I have) spelled/spelt
to spill	(I) spilled/spilt	(I have) spilled/spilt
to spoil	(I) spoiled/spoilt	(I have) spoiled/spoilt

> ⚠ **Watch out for *bought* and *brought***
>
> Some people use *bought*, the past participle of *to buy*, when they mean *brought*, the past participle of *to bring*. Remembering the *r* in *bring* should help you get it right.
>
> I bought the newspaper at the shop and brought it home.

Irregular verbs

Sadly, not all English verbs obey the rules. The many that don't – the bane of language students everywhere – are known as *irregular* verbs. Overleaf is a list of the most common.

The irregular verb people most often get wrong is *to do*.

    I done the washing.   **✗**

The correct forms of the past tense are

    I did the washing.   **✓**

    I have done the washing.   **✓**

Infinitive	Past tense	Past participle
to be	(I) was	(I have) been
to bring	(I) brought	(I have) brought
to buy	(I) bought	(I have) bought
to choose	(I) chose	(I have) chosen
to come	(I) came	(I have) come
to do	(I) did	(I have) done
to drink	(I) drank	(I have) drunk
to eat	(I) ate	(I have) eaten
to go	(I) went	(I have) gone
to grow	(I) grew	(I have) grown
to lie	(I) lay/laid	(I have) laid
to light	(I) lit/lighted	(I have) lit
to mistake	(I) mistook	(I have) mistaken
to read	(I) read	(I have) read
to see	(I) saw	(I have) seen
to sing	(I) sang	(I have) sung
to swim	(I) swam	(I have) swum
to teach	(I) taught	(I have) taught
to write	(I) wrote	(I have) written

> ⚠ **Watch out for *hung* and *hanged***
> If you are talking about hanging a thing, use *hung*.
>   He hung the picture on the wall.
> If you are talking about hanging a person, use *hanged*.
>   They hanged him at dawn.

Forming present and past participles of regular verbs

As we have already seen, the present participle is formed by adding *-ing* to the end of the infinitive. The past participle of regular verbs is formed by adding *-d* or *-ed*.

Infinitive	Present participle	Past participle
to look	looking	looked
to double-cross	double-crossing	double-crossed

However, different rules must be applied in some cases to ensure correct spelling and pronunciation.

Words ending with a short vowel followed by a single consonant

Double the final consonant and add the suffix.

to stop	stopping	stopped
to fit	fitting	fitted
to quarrel	quarrelling	quarrelled
to confer	conferring	conferred

Remember that this does not apply to words ending in *w, x* or *y* as these never appear in doubled form.

Words ending in e
Drop the *e,* then add the suffix.

Infinitive	Present participle	Past participle
to poke	poking	poked
to force	forcing	forced
to contemplate	contemplating	contemplated

⚠ **Watch out for exceptions to the -ing rule**
In a few cases, words ending in *e* simply add the *-ing* without dropping the *e,* in order to avoid ambiguity in the meaning. For example, *dyeing* (from *to dye*) is not the same as *dying* (from to *die*). You should also leave the final *e* on words that rely on it for their pronunciation (*hoeing*).

Both *ageing* and *aging* are correct, although the former is more common in UK usage.

Nouns

Nouns are 'name' words. There are four types: *common nouns, proper nouns, abstract nouns* and *collective nouns.* Nouns can be either the subjects or objects of verbs (see Building Sentences on page 45).

Common nouns
These are simply the names of ordinary things.

> dog, girl, tree, house, plate, car

Proper nouns
These are specific names of places, people and special things. They always start with a capital letter.

> Mary, London, France, Dumbo, Microsoft

Abstract nouns
These are names of intangible things like feelings, ideas, states of mind or measurement.

> happiness, ambition, equality, height, innocence, colour

Collective nouns
These are names for groups of things.

> flock, herd, audience, band, assortment, family

Collective nouns are always considered as a single whole – even though they may be made up of lots of individual members – so they take the singular form of the verb in a sentence.

> The audience **was** delighted with the performance.

> The family that **eats** together, **stays** together.

Many nouns have a specific collective noun that should be used with them. The list overleaf gives some of the most common.

a bale of cotton/hay/wood
a band of musicians
a batch of biscuits/cakes, etc.
a bevy of beauties
a board of directors
a bouquet of flowers
a brood of hens
a bunch of grapes
a choir of singers
a cluster of diamonds
a clutch of eggs
a company of actors
a fleet of cars/ships
a flight of stairs/steps
a flotilla of boats
a gaggle of geese
a galaxy of stars
a hand of bananas
a herd of cows
a host of angels
a litter of kittens/puppies
a nest of vipers
a pack of wolves
a pride of lions
a school of whales/dolphins
a sheaf of corn/wheat
a shoal of fish

Gender

Nouns fall into four gender groups.

Masculine for male people and animals

man, earl, bull

Feminine for female people and animals

woman, duchess, cow

Common for words denoting people or animals that can be of either sex

child, tenant, fish

Neuter for words denoting things with no sex

book, shoe, feather

⚠ **Watch out for saying *he or she***

When the gender of something is common or unspecified (such as *individual, tenant,* etc.) it used to be correct to use the pronoun *he* or *his* when referring to the person. In today's world of increasing political correctness and sexual equality, this is no longer considered acceptable. There are various approaches to the problem. Using *she* and *her* all the time may prove some sort of point but can be very confusing. Repeated use of *he or she* can become annoying and *(s)he* is ugly and unpronounceable. The best solution is to rework the sentence to avoid the phrase altogether. If this is not possible, choose one gender and use it consistently. The following is part of an agreement prepared for a landlord of student houses and was handed out even when all the tenants were girls!

> Each tenant is required to give one week's notice or he will be charged an extra week's rent. If he wishes to extend his tenancy, he must inform me in writing or I shall not allow him to stay.

It may be appropriate to put a note at the beginning of the passage, giving your reason for choosing *he* instead of *she* or vice versa.

Articles

The, a and *an* are known as *articles*. They always precede a noun.

The is called the *definite article* because it is specific. When you write *the man,* you are not referring to just any man – you are indicating one particular man.

A and *an* are called *indefinite articles* because they are non-specific. You should use *a* when it precedes a word that starts with a consonant (a parasol, a piano) and *an* when the word starts with a vowel (an umbrella, an upright piano).

⚠ Watch out for *a hotel*

You may hear people use *an* with words beginning with *h*. This is only correct if the *h* is silent. In the past, *hotel* was pronounced as *'otel* so it was correct to use *an hotel*. Nowadays we say *hotel*, so *a hotel* is correct.

I am going to stay the night at a hotel.

You still use *an* for words that have a silent *h* – they nearly all relate to the words *heir, honour* and *honest*:

He died without leaving an heir.

She has an honest face.

He was an honourable man.

Pronouns

Pronouns are used instead of nouns in a sentence so that you don't need to keep repeating the noun itself.

Personal pronouns

These are the little words that are used to replace proper nouns – such as *Mary* – or common nouns with an article – such as *a cat* – where you want to avoid repeating the noun.

> Mary slapped James. **She** slapped **him** twice.
>
> The blows were extremely hard. **They** reduced **him** to tears.

Personal pronouns come in pairs: *I/me, you/you, he/him, she/her, it/it, we/us, they/them.*

It is usually very clear which form to use.

> **I** like food.
>
> **You** go to the shops.
>
> **We** hate scary movies.
>
> **They** live in a city.
>
> The baby smiled at **me**.
>
> He loves **her**.
>
> The book was given to **them**.

I and me

Some people become confused when there is more than one person involved. For example, should you say *My friend and I like going to parties* or *My friend and me like going to parties*? To decide which is right, simply split up the two people in the sentence.

> **My friend** likes going to parties.
>
> *I* also like going to parties.

Therefore, the complete sentence should be:

> My friend and *I* like going to parties.

Now look at this example. *The taxi driver gave my friend and I/me a lift.* Divide it as before.

> The taxi driver gave **my friend** a lift.
>
> The taxi driver also gave **me** a lift.

Therefore, the complete sentence should be:

> The taxi driver gave my friend and **me** a lift.

⚠ Watch out for *me and my friend*

Note that you should always put yourself second, so you should say *my friend and me* (or *my friend and I* if that's correct), not *me and my friend*. Remember, even the Queen puts herself second in this case. She always says: 'My husband and I'.

⚠ **Watch out for *between you and I***

This is a common mistake – it should **always** be *between you and me*. If you're not sure why it's wrong, think of the pronouns as a pair: *you and I* means *we*; *you and me* means *us*. Put like that, *between you and I* becomes *between we*, which is clearly wrong.

This rule applies to all prepositions (see page 38).

Myself

Myself has two definite jobs in a sentence.

It may be used to show that you are doing something to yourself.

> I cut myself shaving.
>
> I cried myself to sleep.

It may also be used to emphasise a point.

> Myself, I prefer plain chocolates.
>
> I'll do it myself.

It should **never** be used instead of *me* or *I* but its misuse is becoming more and more common, in sentences such as these.

> You can write to any one of the team, including myself. ✗
>
> My aunt invited myself and my family to spend a week in Wales. ✗
>
> Myself and my friends went to Ibiza. ✗

Here are the correct versions.

> You can write to any one of the team, including me.   ✓
> My aunt invited my family and me to spend a week in Wales. ✓
> My friends and I went to Ibiza.   ✓

In the same way, *ourselves* should never be used instead of *we* or *us*.

> There will be a meeting between ourselves and the
> directors next week.   ✗
> There will be a meeting between the directors and us
> next week.   ✓

⚠ **Watch out for *theirselves***
Some people say *theirselves* when they mean *themselves*.
There is **no such word** as *theirselves* so *themselves* is always the correct choice.

This and that, these and those

These little words (and sometimes *they*) are called *demonstrative pronouns* because they demonstrate, or show, that something is either the subject or object of the sentence.

In these examples, they are the subject of the verb in the sentence.

> This is a good place to stop.
> That was a delicious lunch.
> These are the best strawberries I have ever tasted.
> Those boys were causing the trouble.

In these examples, they are the object of the verb in the sentence.

> I need this.
> Don't do that.
> He wants these.
> Give me one of those.

⚠ **Watch out for** *Those are them*

Many people say *Those are them* or, even more incorrectly, *That's them*, but, strictly speaking, you should say *Those are they*. If you think that sounds stilted, say *There they are* instead!

Who and whom

These are *interrogative pronouns*, so-called because they are used to introduce questions. They are not interchangeable: *who* is used as the subject of a sentence that asks a question and *whom* as the object of a verb within the question.

If you are unsure of which to use, imagine a likely answer to the question. If the answer contains *I, he, she, we* or *they*, then the question should use *who*.

> Question: Who hid behind the bush?
> (Answer: **They** hid behind the bush.)

If the answer to the question is likely to be *me, him, her, us* or *them*, then you should use *whom*.

> Question: To whom did you give the money?
> (Answer: I gave the money to **him**.)

> **⚠ Watch out for *it* and *you***
> *It* and *you* do not change whatever the question and answer so, if you are unsure, use *who*. In practice, very few people actually use *whom* in spoken English so it is unlikely that anyone will notice!

Which and what

These are also *interrogative pronouns,* used when asking questions about things.

Which is used when asking for choice from a definite set of options.

> Which do you prefer – butter or margarine?

What is used when asking for a choice from a range of unknown possibilities.

> What are you holding?

Whose and who's

Whose is a *relative pronoun* denoting ownership. In a way, it means *to whom it belongs.*

> There is the man whose car I borrowed.

Who's is a contraction, or shortening, of *who is* or *who has*. It is common in spoken English but you should not use it in formal writing. Use the full form instead.

> Who's that man lurking in the shadows?

See also Apostrophes, page 53.

Adjectives

Adjectives are 'describing' words. They are used to tell you more about a noun. Words that describe colour, shape, size, age, texture, nationality, disposition, etc. are all adjectives.

>   the big red ball
>   the angry old man
>   an elegant French sofa

Compound adjectives

As you might expect, these are formed when two adjectives link together into one. They always contain a hyphen.

>   the black-bearded man
>   the 20-mile hike

The purpose of the hyphen is to avoid ambiguity. Without the hyphen, you could have two different meanings. In the example above, *the black, bearded man* would not be the same as *the black-bearded man*.

See also Hyphens, page 65.

Comparative and superlative adjectives

These are used when making comparisons between things.

When you are comparing two similar or identical things, you use a *comparative adjective*.

>   My dog is bigger than yours.

When you are comparing three or more things, you use a *superlative adjective*.

This is the prettiest dress of all.

Forming comparative and superlative adjectives

It is quite simple to form the comparative and superlative forms of any adjective.

If the adjective has only one syllable, add -*er* to the adjective to make the comparative and -*est* to make the superlative. In this way, from *young* you can form *younger* and, *youngest* and from *old* you get *older* and *oldest*.

He was the younger of the two brothers.

Gemma was the oldest girl in the class.

If there is a single vowel before the last consonant, you double the last letter before adding the -*er* or -*est*.

big, bigger, biggest

thin, thinner, thinnest

This does not apply if the last consonant is *w* or *y*, as these are never doubled.

low, lower, lowest

gay, gayer, gayest

If the adjective has two syllables and ends in -*y*, change the -*y* to -*i*, then add -*er* or -*est*.

happy, happier, happiest

funny, funnier, funniest

For most other two-syllable adjectives and all those with three or more syllables, you simply put *more* or *most* with the adjective.

> dangerous, more dangerous, most dangerous
> helpful, more helpful, most helpful

As ever, there are some words that simply don't follow the rules. These you just have to learn.

> bad, worse, worst
> far, farther, farthest
> good, better, best
> little, less, least
> much/many, more, most
> clever, cleverer, cleverest

See also Beginnings and Endings of Words, starting on page 179.

⚠ Watch out for *fewer*
Fewer follows the rules for comparative adjectives, but many people use it incorrectly and confuse it with *less*. See page 119 for a full explanation.

Complete adjectives

There are a few adjectives whose meaning is complete in itself and these should never be put into a comparative or superlative context. Instead, you should rephrase your sentence.

Unique: This means the *only one of its kind*. By definition, therefore, something cannot be *more unique* and certainly not *the most unique of all*!

Complete: A task or thing is either complete – finished, or whole – or it is not. The following example may be quite common in spoken English but it is wrong.

> That is the most complete mess I have ever seen. ✗

Empty: If a container is empty, there is nothing inside. It cannot be made more or less empty.

> This jug is emptier than that one. ✗
>
> There is less in this jug than in that one. ✓

However, used figuratively, it can mean *hollow* and in that case a comparative is possible.

> After her husband died, her life felt emptier than ever before.

Full: There are no degrees of fullness – a container is either full or it is not.

> Can you make this cup of tea fuller? ✗
>
> Can you put more in this cup of tea? ✓

However, the word may be used comparatively when it is used in a figurative sense.

> She described her experiences in the fullest detail.

Extreme: Strictly speaking, this refers to the outermost or farthest point.

> She went to extreme lengths to prevent her husband from finding her money. (She could go no further.)

However, it may also be used to mean immoderate or lacking restraint, in which case a comparative is possible.

> We are both on the right wing of the party, but his views on the punishment of criminals are a great deal more extreme than mine.

Verbal adjectives

Present and past participles of many verbs may be used as active describing words.

> the roaring fire
>
> the shocked woman

In this form they are often placed at the beginning of sentences, to give prominence to the idea they convey.

> Roaring in the grate, the fire gave out an intense heat.
>
> Shocked, the woman sat down, her hands clasped in her lap.

Be careful how you do this: it's easy to put the verbal adjective in the wrong place in the sentence and give a completely different meaning.

> Barbecued in the open, children love chicken and sausages. ✗

Set like this, the sentence implies the children are being barbecued, not the chicken and sausages! The correct order is

> Children love chicken and sausages barbecued in the open. ✓

Adverbs

Adverbs are words that give you more information about particular words in a sentence. Adverbs are usually made up of adjectives with *-ly* on the end (*see* Beginnings and Endings of Words, page 179).

Adverbs are used most often to refer to verbs and to describe in more detail how the action is being carried out – in what manner, when, where, how often.

> *The wind blew strongly.*
>
> *The girl ran quickly.*
>
> *His voice faltered momentarily.*

⚠ **Watch out for using adjectives instead of adverbs**

When describing a verb, you must use an adverb.

He ate his meal too quick.	✗
He ate his meal too quickly.	✓

Sometimes the same word can be both an adjective and an adverb.

In this sentence, *fast* is an adjective.

> *He drove a fast car.*

In this sentence, it is an adverb.

> *He drove fast.*

If you don't know whether you need an adjective or an adverb, try substituting another word that means the same. In the next example, we have changed *fast* to *speedy*. The sentence that contains the adverb becomes clear, as it needs a little adjustment.

> He drove a speedy car.
>
> He drove **speedily**.

Adverbs can also be used to qualify adjectives. It is important that you put them in the correct place in a sentence to convey the meaning that you want.

In this example, the adverb *dangerously* is describing the verb *skidded*.

> The car skidded dangerously on the icy road.

In this example, the adverb is describing the adjective *icy*.

> The car skidded on the dangerously icy road.

⚠ **Watch out for positioning adverbs correctly**

If you position the adverb wrongly, it can make complete nonsense of a sentence. The first example below implies that the repairs should be carried out badly!

> The roof needs repairing badly.　　　　　　　✗
>
> The roof badly needs repairing.　　　　　　　✓

Tortured adverbs

I have said that adverbs are formed by adding *-ly* to the end of adjectives. This holds true in most cases but if you use the rule with compound adjectives, you will end up with quite a mouthful. Made-up words such as *mind-bogglingly, long-sufferingly, blood-curdlingly,* etc. are called *tortured adverbs*.

Strictly speaking, there is nothing wrong with them but they sound ludicrous and are difficult to say. A better alternative would be a well-chosen adjective or a complete rearrangement of the phrase – especially in written English.

> *Watching the horror movie was sick-makingly horrible.* ✗
> *Watching the horror movie was horrible and sick-making.* ✓

Prepositions

These are the little words that usually go before nouns and pronouns to show how they link to the rest of the sentence.

after	*against*
along	*amid/amidst*
among/amongst	*around*
at	*before*
behind	*below*
beneath	*beside*
between	*beyond*
by	*down*
during	*except*
for	*from*
in	*inside*
into	*near*
of	*off*
on	*outside*
over	*past*
round	*since*

through	to
towards	under
underneath	until
up	upon
with	within
without	

Here are examples of how prepositions are used in sentences.

He gave the chocolates **to** *his girlfriend.*

They both stood **under** *the umbrella.*

There is a new bridge **over** *the river.*

The bill was paid **by** *my uncle.*

Where a preposition is followed by a pronoun, you should always use *me, him, her, us* and *them*. This may seem obvious with only one pronoun – *beside me, after her,* etc. – but many people make mistakes when there is more than one pronoun involved, especially *you and me*.

Apart from you and **me**, *no one seemed to enjoy the meal.*

See also Between You and Me, page 27.

With some words, it is important to use the right preposition in order to give the correct meaning. Here are a few of the most common examples.

> agree **to** (something)
> agree **with** (someone)
> bored **with**
> comply **with**
> deficient **in**
> different **from**
> divide **among** (many things)
> divide **between** (two things)
> equal **to**
> inspired **by**
> protest **at**
> opposite **to**
> similar **to**

Different from and similar to

These two expressions cause many mistakes in English.

Different from is correct because, technically, things that are different are in opposition, so they can be described as moving away **from** each other.

> *The house was different from the apartment.*

Similar to is correct because, conversely, if things are similar, they are close **to** each other.

> *Simon looked very similar to his younger brother.*

Prepositions at the end of sentences

In formal English grammar, it used to be considered wrong to finish a sentence with a preposition:

She wished she had brought a purse to put her change in.

However, the alternative may actually sound worse.

She wished she had brought a purse in which to put her change.

On the whole, in modern language usage, it's perfectly acceptable to put the preposition at the end of a sentence if it sounds better that way. This is especially true if you are asking a question. Look at the examples below: it is doubtful if you would actually use the first – strictly correct – version.

For what are you doing that?

What are you doing that for?

Conjunctions

These are the little words that join words, phrases, clauses and sentences together. They are vital for creating the general sense of the sentence. The most common ones are:

although	and
as	because
but	for
if	or
since	while/whilst

Conjunctions at the beginning of sentences

It used to be considered wrong to start a sentence with *and* or *but* and many people still adhere to this rule. But nowadays we tend to write shorter sentences, so it is considered more acceptable (as in this sentence). If you are writing formally, you may prefer to use a longer sentence or start the sentence with *however*, as in the example below.

> However, nowadays we tend to write shorter sentences, so it is considered more acceptable.

⚠ **Watch out for *and* or *but* starting a paragraph**
It is not good style to start a paragraph with *and* or *but*. A new paragraph should indicate that you are moving on to a different topic, so there should be no reason to link two paragraphs with a conjunction.

All the other conjunctions may be used to start a sentence. This is because it is possible to reverse the order of the clauses that make up the sentence.

> **If** you invite that woman here, I shall go out.
> I shall go out **if** you invite that woman here.
> **From** the look on her face, it was clear she was angry.
> It was clear she was angry **from** the look on her face.

Chapter 2
Sentences and Punctuation

Sentences are made up by grouping together the parts of speech described in the last chapter. However, there are many ways to arrange these groups. In this chapter we shall look at how to build clear, well-constructed sentences. (If, as you read this chapter, you can't remember the meaning of any of the parts of speech, simply turn to the reference list on page 7.)

Every sentence you write should start with a capital letter and end with a full stop and however short and simple it may be, every sentence **must** have a verb.

> I hate you.
>
> Go away.
>
> Leave!

Unless the sentence consists of just one or two words, it will almost certainly contain nouns. The *subject noun* is the person, place or thing doing the action. The *object noun* is the person, place or thing on the receiving end of the action. In the first sentence above, *I* is the subject noun, *hate* is the verb and *you* is the object noun.

Concord

The subject noun and the verb must agree. By this, I mean that if the subject of the verb (the person or thing doing the action) is singular, then the verb must also be singular.

He/she/it/the cat **is**

If the subject noun is plural, then the verb must be plural.

They/the cats **are**

This is called concord.

Check which word is the subject

There are several expressions that many people wrongly use with the plural form of the verb when the verb should take the singular form because it actually refers to one person in a group, not the whole group. To check, add *one* to the sentence.

Each of the girls have a new dress.	✗
Each of the girls has a new dress.	✓

If you add *one*, the mistake becomes obvious:

Each one of the girls have a new dress.	✗
Each one of the girls has a new dress.	✓

This rule applies to the following expressions.

None of *the men has a reason to be here.*

Either of *us is happy to help.*

Every one of *the musicians plays two instruments.*

Neither of *the boys enjoys football.*

None of *the group was injured.*

Not one of the glasses was broken.

One of the children hits the ball.

Has **any of** these exam papers been marked?

One and one makes two

When two subjects are joined together with *and,* they become the joint subject of the sentence and therefore take the plural form of the verb. This applies whether the subjects themselves are singular or plural.

The cat and the mouse **are** afraid of each other.

The pans and the kettle **are** kept in the cupboard.

Building sentences

Now we are going to learn, step by step, how to construct sentences. To make things more interesting, the sentences in the examples are linked together to form a little narrative.

A sentence may consist of just one word, as long as that word is a verb.

'Listen!'

However, usually a sentence consists of a verb and a subject noun, with or without an article. The subject noun must always agree with the verb.

The	door	opened.
ARTICLE	SUBJECT NOUN	VERB

You can then add more detail by attaching an adjective to the noun or an adverb to the verb.

The oak door opened slowly.

ADJECTIVE ADVERB

Next, you might join two clauses together with a conjunction.

The oak door opened slowly and a man crept into the room.

CONJUNCTION

You can now introduce pronouns referring to the nouns you have already introduced.

He shut it silently behind him.

PRONOUN PRONOUN

Punctuation

So far we have used short, simple sentences. If you wish to build up sentences that are any more complicated, you have to introduce punctuation marks. These will add expression and clarity to your sentences. Without it, the sentences will be dull and probably incomprehensible. We have already mentioned the full stop at the end of the sentence; here are the other punctuation marks.

comma	,
quotation marks	"double" and 'single'
apostrophe	'
exclamation mark	!
ellipsis	...
question mark	?

semi-colon	;
colon	:
brackets	(round) and [square]
dash	—
hyphen	-

Commas

Commas provide breaks or pauses within a sentence. The breaks are lighter than those provided by a full stop but it is best not to insert too many as they can upset the flow of the sentence. Commas can be used in several different ways.

To separate adjectives: If there is a list of two or more adjectives describing the subject or object, commas may be used to separate them.

> A roaring log fire flickered in the enormous, ornate, cast-iron grate.

To enclose descriptive phrases: You can use a comma to separate a phrase from the rest of the sentence. Remember, a phrase, unlike a clause, does not include a verb, it is simply added information:

> A woman, aged about 30, sat with her back to the door.

To separate items in a list: This is the same idea as the list of adjectives above, but the items may be quite long.

> She was adorned with expensive jewellery that included a solid gold watch, three gold chains, a heavy gold bracelet, diamond earrings, several rings and a diamond hair-clasp.

You should not use a comma before a simple conjunction such as *and* and *but*, so in the last example there's no need for a comma before the last item in a list. However, if the sense is ambiguous, you can add the comma to clarify the meaning. In the next example, the final comma makes it clear that Fortnum and Mason is one shop and Selfridges is another.

> In her hand she was clutching bills from Harrods, Fortnum and Mason, and Selfridges.

To separate clauses: You can use a comma to separate clauses in a sentence. (Remember, a clause is a short sentence within a longer sentence. It is complete on its own as it includes a verb. If you take it out, the rest of the sentence should still make sense.)

> Her face was pale, her brow appeared furrowed.

However, you don't need to use a comma if the clauses in a sentence are joined with a conjunction.

> She stared at the bills and shook her head sadly.

When a sentence starts with a conjunction, always insert a comma to separate that clause from the rest of the sentence.

> Because she was lost in thought, she did not hear the door open.

To enclose an aside: Another use of commas is to separate a phrase that is less important than the rest of the sentence (and without which the sentence could still stand alone).

> The room, despite the crackling fire, was cold.

To separate a series of actions or events: Sometimes, you may want to use a series of verbs in a sentence, in which case you need to separate them with commas. This is similar to the use of commas between clauses as described earlier.

> She stood up, sat down, shivered, leant over, picked up her glass and took a long drink of whisky.

To separate an explanatory word or phrase: If an adverb or an explanatory phrase comes within the sentence, it needs a comma before and after it. If the word or phrase comes at the beginning of the sentence, it needs a comma after it.

> The problem was, in fact, she was heavily in debt. However, she had no intention of stopping her spending. Shopping was all she had to do in life.

To clarify meaning: The position of a comma can clarify an ambiguous sentence.

> She knew that the villagers nicknamed her Elizabeth, Queen of the Mall.

Without the comma, her name becomes Elizabeth Queen!

With direct speech in quotation marks: Commas are always used to separate words that are said (this is known as *direct speech*) from the words that indicate the person who said them (*the attribution*). It is important to position the comma correctly.

If the quoted words open the sentence, followed by the attribution, a comma should be placed **inside** the quotation marks.

> 'This is ridiculous,' she muttered.

If the attribution comes first, put the comma **before** the quotation marks.

> Louder than before, she said, 'This is utterly ridiculous.'

Quotation marks

These are also known as *inverted commas*. There are no set rules for when to use "double" or 'single' quotation marks, but you must be consistent. Generally speaking, nowadays more people use single quotation marks. Quotation marks have a variety of uses.

To indicate direct speech: The actual words someone says must always be contained within quotation marks. You can have several sentences within one set of quotation marks if they are all said by the same person. Start each new sentence within the quotation marks with a capital letter.

If the attribution (the words that indicate who is speaking) follows the speech, you should place a comma at the end of the spoken words, **inside** the quotation marks, and the final full stop **after** the attribution.

> 'This is not fair. I don't spend all that much. They can't stop my credit cards,' she almost whimpered.

If the attribution comes within the speech, you have to close the quotation marks before it and open a new set after it. If the direct speech is in two separate sentences, you should place the first full stop after the attribution.

> 'Perhaps I can sell some jewellery to pay them off,' she said more brightly. 'I'll look into it first thing in the morning.'

The two parts of the direct speech can also be phrases or clauses, separated by commas, with a full stop at the end.

> 'After all,' she said, 'there's nothing to worry about really.'

There is no need for a capital letter at the beginning of the second part of the speech when all the spoken words are part of one sentence.

> ⚠ **Watch out for using lower case after closing quotation marks**
> If there is an attribution after the spoken words, as in the last example, there is no need to start it with a capital letter. This is obvious when the speech ends with a comma – as is most usual – but it also applies after a question mark or exclamation mark, as in *'Thank goodness!' she thought.*

When writing conversations between two or more people, it is important to clarify who said what. Always start a new line for each new speaker and remember to open the quotation marks when they start to speak and close them when they have finished.

> She imagined the conversation she would have with the jeweller the following day:
> 'I would like to sell these diamonds. How much are they worth?'
> 'Five thousand pounds, madam.'
> 'Five thousand? Don't be ridiculous!'
> 'Well, perhaps we could offer a little bit more as you're such a good customer. Eight thousand pounds and that's our final offer.'
> 'What if I want to sell the watch as well?' she demanded.
> 'With the watch, ten thousand,' said the jeweller, smiling in a patronising, sickly-sweet manner.

Spoken words can be written as *indirect* or *reported speech*. This is where the reader is told what is or was said, rather than the actual words being reproduced. Indirect speech is usually introduced by the word *that* – *he explained that, she said that, he reported that* and so on. You don't need quotation marks for indirect speech.

> She went on reasoning with herself, saying that she would be able to get a good deal and money would no longer be a problem.

To indicate made-up words: Quotation marks are often used to indicate that a word is in some way not quite appropriate. It may be slang, or a made-up word, or a euphemism.

> She knew she was good at 'blagging' her way out of trouble.

⚠ **Watch out for quotations within quotations**

If you need to use quotation marks around text that is already within quotation marks, use double quotation marks within single quotation marks or vice versa.

> 'I know I'm good at "blagging" my way out of trouble,' she thought.

Around quotations and song titles: If you quote words from another written source, such as a novel or a poem, then obviously they should be contained in quotation marks. Quotation marks should also be used to enclose titles of some things, including names of articles, books, short poems or songs.

She started humming the Abba song 'Money, Money, Money'.
Note that the inverted commas enclose only the title. They don't include the full stop at the end of the sentence.

Apostrophes

Apostrophes are widely misused nowadays. There are only two reasons to insert an apostrophe: to indicate that something belongs to someone or to indicate that some letters are missing.

> ⚠ **Watch out for apostrophes in plurals**
> You should **never** form plural nouns by adding *'s*. So if you see any signs like this when you are out shopping, they are **WRONG!**
> *Fresh carrot's for sale.* ✗

Apostrophes to indicate possession: Placing an apostrophe followed by an *s* at the end of a noun shows that something belongs to that person or thing (*the boy's mother, the baby's bib, the cat's whiskers*). If the noun is single, the apostrophe goes **before** the *s*. In this example, the diamonds belong to Elizabeth.

Elizabeth's diamonds sparkled in the firelight.

If the noun is plural and already ends in *s*, the apostrophe goes after the *s*. In this example, the value belongs to all the diamonds.

The diamonds' value was phenomenal.

> **⚠ Watch out for apostrophes with irregular plurals**
> Remember that nouns such as *children* and *people* are already plural, so in the possessive, the apostrophe must come before the *s*.
> the children's books
> the people's princess

Apostrophes to indicate something is missing: Apostrophes are also used to show that one or more letters or numbers have been left out.

Words with letters missing are known as *contractions*. For example, *didn't* is short for *did not* – the *o* in *not* is left out.

Elizabeth did**n't** realise she was being watched.

In this next example, the *ha* in *had* is left out.

She**'d** become engrossed in her worries. She**'d** also forgotten that her friends, the Walkers, should be arriving soon.

> **⚠ Watch out for *ain't***
> *Ain't* is a colloquialism meaning *am/are/is/has/have not*. Like all slang, it should be avoided in written English unless you want to indicate dialect in direct speech.

The expression *o'clock* is a contraction of the words *of the clock*. A whole word has been missed out and the remainder contracted.

> She glanced at her watch and saw that it was after 9 **o'**clock.
> Henry would be home soon, and she was desperate to
> avoid a row over her debts.

In the following sentence, the number *19* has been left out –
Elizabeth is reminiscing about the *1960s*.

> She wished that she were still living in the carefree **'60**s.

In some expressions, the *a* and *d* are left out of the word *and*.

> Then she'd been a dedicated fan of rock **'n'** roll, and didn't
> even own a credit card.

⚠ **Watch out for** *'n'*

In expressions like fish 'n' chips, wet 'n' wild, bangers 'n'
mash, etc., you must use two apostrophes (' '), not a pair of
single quotation marks (' '). Each apostrophe indicates a
position where one letter is missing.

Its and it's
These two little words often causes confusion but the rules are,
in fact, very simple.

Its (no apostrophe) means *belonging to it* – just as *his or hers*
(which do not have apostrophes!) mean *belonging to him or her.*

> The cat, curled up in front of the fire, stretched out its paws.

It's (with an apostrophe) is a contraction of *it is* – the
apostrophe shows the letter *i* is missing from the word *is*.

> 'It's as I suspected,' thought the man standing just inside
> the door. He turned and slipped silently out of the room.

Apostrophes in words ending in *s*
If a word ending in *s* is a plural, place the apostrophe **after** the *s* (*the girls' faces, the dogs' tails*). In the example below, the noun is plural, referring to Mr and Mrs Walker.

She thought she heard her friends' car in the drive.

Some words ending in *s* are singular (*bus, James*). In this case, add the apostrophe and another *s* (*James's ball, the bus's front wheels*).

She remembered it was Bess's night off.

⚠ **Watch out for apostrophes with collective nouns**
Remember that nouns such as *audience* are singular, so in the possessive, the apostrophe must come before the *s*.
the audience's reaction

Exclamation marks

These are placed at the end of words that are cried out loudly. The exclamation may be a single word, such as a command, or a phrase or sentence. A verb can stand alone as an exclamation, making a complete sentence. (*Stop!*) An exclamation mark acts as a full stop when it is at the end of a sentence so you don't need a full stop as well. Remember to use a capital letter at the beginning of a sentence following an exclamation mark.

Clang! The ancient bell on the front door rang. She rushed into the hall, exclaiming, 'Oh my goodness!'

See also Full Stops, page 57, and Capital Letters, page 194.

⚠ **Watch out for using too many exclamation marks**
Use exclamation marks sparingly. Using one at the end of every sentence will give your writing a jerky and rather irritating appearance and style. Never use more than one at the end of a sentence, unless you are writing something very informal, such as a letter to a close friend.

Full stops

Full stops are used to complete sentences and also to indicate abbreviations.

Full stops at the end of sentences: You already know that full stops are used to end all sentences. By using them to break up short sentences, rather than using longer ones, you can add impact and change the pace of the writing. Here it adds a note of menace.

> The door stood ajar. Mist swirled in. No one was there.
> Night had fallen.

Compare this to the next example, which uses commas and conjunctions instead of some of the full stops. This gives a lighter tone to the words.

> The door stood ajar, mist swirled in and no one was there.
> Night had fallen.

Full stops in abbreviations: Full stops should be placed at the end of abbreviations.

e.g.	Wed. (Wednesday)
H.G. Wells	p. 9 (page 9)
Ph.D. (doctor of philosophy)	Woods and Co.

Full stops are **not** used when the abbreviated word begins and ends with the same letter as the whole word.

Mrs (originally Mistress)	St (Saint)
Mr (Mister)	Revd (Reverend)
Ms (Miss or Mistress)	Ltd (Limited)
Dr (Doctor)	

Full stops are also no longer considered necessary in *acronyms* – words formed from the initial letters of the actual name that are pronounced as words in their own right.

AIDS

BAFTA

They are also not used in common or colloquial abbreviations.

co-op

demo

decaf

See also Abbreviations, page 192.

Ellipses

This is the technical word for three spaced full stops, also sometimes known as *omission marks*. An ellipsis is used to indicate a word or series of words is missing from the text.

Use an ellipsis if you are copying a extract from a book, play, article or other piece of writing and you don't want to use the whole piece. Insert the three dots wherever something has been left out. Here is an example of whole text followed by a shortened version, with parts left out.

> She re-read the scribbled note that Bess had left by the telephone:
>
> 'Dear Madam, I will be back tomorrow in time to make breakfast as usual. I am so sorry for the inconvenience. The Walkers phoned and asked me to tell you that they have been delayed in Woolington so they won't be with you in time for dinner. They still hope to come over anyway but if they're not there by 9.30, they'll come another day.'

> '... Back tomorrow in time to make breakfast ...Walkers phoned ... delayed ... if they're not there by 9.30, they'll come another day.'

You can also use an ellipsis at the end of a sentence, to indicate that there might be more to come. This device is often used to add suspense.

> Elizabeth was sure she hadn't imagined the doorbell. She stared out into the night ...

Question marks

A question mark must be placed at the end of any direct question, whether in speech or prose.

> 'Meg, John, are you there?' she called out, nervously. What could be scarier than finding the front door open, with no one there, and being sure you heard a car draw up and the door bell ring?

You don't need a question mark when using indirect speech (see page 52).

> She asked nervously if her friends were there.

Semi-colons

These can be used in two ways.

To create a noticeable pause: Semi-colons, like commas, may be used to break up sentences. You can link two clauses with a semi-colon without the need for a conjunction. This gives a longer pause than a comma, but shorter than if you separated the text into two sentences.

> She shut the door; it was eerily quiet in the dark hall.

To separate long items in a list: Semi-colons can also be used instead of commas to separate items in a list. This is very useful when the items are long and already contain commas.

> She went back to the lounge and grabbed her glass; the half-empty bottle of whisky; her cashmere pashmina, which was thrown over the back of the armchair, and a copy of Vogue magazine.

Colons

Colons should not be confused with semi-colons. Their primary function is to introduce, or herald, a piece of text. Colons have several specific purposes.

To precede an explanation: The text after a colon expands on what is said at the beginning of the sentence.

> The clock struck 10 o'clock. There was no point in waiting:
> the Walkers wouldn't be coming now.

To introduce a quotation or an example: Here, the colon precedes the title of the magazine article.

> She glanced at the magazine. A question on the cover made
> her smile: 'Are you bored with your wealth?'

To introduce a list: The list following the comma details all the things that bore Elizabeth. Note that the text referring to her wealth must be set in a separate sentence – it is not part of the list of boring things.

> There were lots of things with which she was bored: her
> home, her husband, her lifestyle and her loneliness. However,
> she was certainly not bored with her wealth!

To introduce direct speech: A colon can be used instead of a comma when the attribution precedes the speech.

> She shouted out loud: 'I'm sick of all this!'

To introduce dialogue in a play manuscript: In written dialogue, the name of the person speaking is followed by a colon, then their speech.

> She climbed the stairs, swaying slightly, imagining the scenario that would follow when Henry found out.
> **Elizabeth:** Darling, there's been a mistake. I've made a tiny miscalculation.
> **Henry** [staring at the bills]: How can you stand there and say that £10,000 is a miscalculation? Are you completely mad or just plain stupid?
> **Elizabeth:** Please don't be angry.
> **Henry** [bellowing]: I have every right to be angry! What kind of wife...?

⚠ **Watch out for capital letters after a colon**
You must use a capital letter after a colon only when you are writing direct speech.

Brackets
Round brackets
Also called *parentheses,* these are used when you add extra information but want to keep it separate. Round brackets and their contents may form part of a longer sentence. If this is the case, you don't use a capital letter or a full stop to start and finish the text in the brackets, but you do put a question mark or exclamation mark, if appropriate.

> Elizabeth sat on the bed, drank the rest of the whisky (her
> headache in the morning would be dreadful!) and lay down.

Sometimes, the text inside the brackets may form a whole sentence, starting with a capital letter and ending with a full stop

> She didn't move but she was acutely aware of the silence.
> (She was also a little afraid now.) What had happened to
> her friends and why was she so alone?

Square brackets

These are much less common than round brackets. They are used mainly to enclose words that are not actually part of the original text but have been added by someone other than the original writer or speaker in order to make the meaning clear.

> Her head was beginning to hurt. 'They [the Walkers] should
> have come,' she thought miserably.

You will frequently see square brackets in newspapers and magazines where someone's words are being quoted but have been changed slightly for the purposes of the article. They can also be used instead of round brackets to add special types of information, such as stage directions (see the example in the dialogue on page 62).

Dashes

Dashes are used frequently in informal, everyday writing but less often in formal writing. They have several uses.

To separate a clause: Dashes can be used in the same way as commas or brackets to separate a clause from the rest of a sentence.

> Head and heart pounding – and very drunk now – she fell into a deep sleep.

To replace a colon before a list: A dash may be used instead of a colon to precede a list.

> She had a frightening, muddled dream, with everything swirling round in her mind – diamonds, a black shadowy figure, pain, mist and relief.

A dash may also be placed after a list, introducing the explanation for the list.

> Her money worries, her love of shopping, her guilt and her boredom – all these emotions were going round and round in her head.

To show hesitation in speech: A dash can be used to convey the pauses people make when talking.

> 'I – er – wish – oh, I – I can't bear this!' she whispered to herself.

To indicate an afterthought: In this case, the dash shows that the final thought is an afterthought, or a condition on which the rest of the sentence depends.

> The Walkers stood on the front doorstep and rang the bell. They were hoping for a coffee and a chat – if Elizabeth was still awake.

To create a pause before a climax: In written text, a dash may be used to indicate a dramatic pause, such as you would make if you were reading aloud.

> *The front door stood open and a light was on upstairs.*
> *Calling out, they went up to Elizabeth's bedroom. She lay sprawled on the bed – dead.*

Hyphens

Hyphens look like short dashes. They are used in a variety of ways.

To join a word that breaks between two lines: If there is not enough room at the end of a line for a complete word, you can 'break' it, joining the two sections with a hyphen. Try to break words at the end of a syllable and not too near the beginning or end of the word, but take care that you split the word correctly. For instance, *manslaughter* should be split into *man-slaughter*, not *mans-laughter*! If the word is already hyphenated, break it at the original hyphen. Words with only one syllable cannot be hyphenated.

> *Meg and John stood frozen to the spot. Elizabeth was im-maculately made-up and fully clothed but had no jewel-lery. Even her rings, which she always wore, were miss-ing. She reeked of whisky.*

⚠ **Watch out for hyphens at the end of lines**
Always put the hyphen after the first part of the word at the
end of the first line, not before the second part of the word
at the beginning of the second line.

To link numbers together: Hyphens may be used with words or
numbers that are linked in some way.

> John grabbed the phone by the bed and dialled 9-9-9. They
> went downstairs to the lounge to wait for the police. The
> clock said twenty-past-eleven.

To join two words to create one: Hyphens used in this way help
to avoid any ambiguity. In the example below, *a wad of
50-pound notes,* where each note is worth £50, is worth far
more than *a wad of 50 pound notes,* where each of the notes is
worth £1.

> On the table lay the pile of bills, topped with a wad of
> 50-pound notes.
>
> 'Jumping jack-in-the-box!' whistled John. 'That's a lot of cash.'

Omitting the hyphen may completely change the meaning.

> John wondered secretly if Elizabeth had been having an
> extra-marital affair.

In this case, if you remove the hyphen (*John wondered secretly
if Elizabeth had been having an extra marital affair*), John would
be wondering if Elizabeth was having another marital affair.

See also Prefixes, page 179.

Arranging complex sentences

Most complex sentences can be arranged in different ways without altering the meaning. When writing a sentence, you should always choose the arrangement that flows best and avoids ambiguity.

Consider the following sentence. It is easy to understand, despite being quite long.

> John and Meg sat in the lounge wondering why Elizabeth was dead, what had happened to her that evening and where all the money had come from.

This next version sounds rather stilted.

> In the lounge sat John and Meg wondering where all the money had come from, what had happened to Elizabeth that evening and why she was dead.

This final example is ambiguous – and incorrect – because it sounds as though the money arrived while they were in the lounge.

> John and Meg wondered what had happened to Elizabeth, why she was dead and where all the money had come from while they sat in the lounge.

Paragraphs

Breaking up text into paragraphs makes it easier to follow. A paragraph is simply a sequence of sentences with a common theme that runs through the whole passage. When deciding where to stop and start your paragraphs, the rule is simple: just start a new paragraph for each new point.

In written text, line spaces may be left between paragraphs. Each new paragraph may also be indented.

Paragraphs can vary in length enormously. They may be just one sentence – a device often used to give impact to text. Alternatively, they may run to as much as several pages. However, for easy reading, it is best not to make them too long.

The police arrived and soon the house was swarming with detectives and forensic experts. An inspector took statements from Meg and John, who could give him very few clues as to what had gone on that evening. The couple went over everything that had happened: about being late; hoping to find Elizabeth up so they could have a drink and a chat; finding her dead, awash with alcohol; the fact that all her jewellery had gone; the bills and, strangest of all, the money. Why would a thief leave so much cash and yet steal jewellery?

The detectives wanted to know where Elizabeth's husband and the members of household staff were. Meg and John were able to tell them that it was the housekeeper's night off but that they didn't know where Henry was. Usually Elizabeth said when he was away on business, but this time she hadn't.

As the clock struck midnight, nobody saw the shadowy figure slip out into the night.

Chapter 3
Changing Words from Singular to Plural

Common nouns are either singular (when there is just one thing) or plural (when there are more than one). Most common words add *-s* or *-es* to turn singular into plural but there are many variations, depending on their singular endings.

⚠ **Watch out for matching the noun to the verb**
Remember that if you use a singular noun, the verb must also be singular – or both must be plural (*see* Concord, page 44).

Ways to form plurals
For most singular nouns, you simply add an *s* to the word to make it plural.

Singular	Plural
bag	bags
alibi	alibis
allowance	allowances
tunnel	tunnels
zoo	zoos

There are, however, a number of exceptions.

Words that end in a sibilant

When a singular word ends in a sibilant, you should add *-es* to make the plural. The sibilants are *s, ss, x* and *sh*. This rule also applies to words ending in *-ch*.

Singular	Plural
box	boxes
brush	brushes
clutch	clutches
gas	gases (US gasses)
moss	mosses

Words that end in -is

If a singular word ends in *-is,* it is changed to *-es* (pronounced 'eez') in the plural.

Singular	Plural
analysis	analyses
axis	axes
crisis	crises
diagnosis	diagnoses
hypothesis	hypotheses
parenthesis	parentheses
synopsis	synopses
thesis	theses

Words that end in -y

These fall into two categories: those that end in a *y* preceded by a vowel (*boy, day*) and those that end in a *y* preceded by a consonant (*gallery, nanny*).

If the letter before the final *y* is a vowel, just add *s* to make the plural form.

Singular	Plural
play	plays
monkey	monkeys
valley	valleys
toy	toys
guy	guys

If the letter before the final *y* is a consonant, change the *y* to *i* and add *-es* to make the plural form.

Singular	Plural
ruby	rubies
caddy	caddies
fly	flies
army	armies
penny	pennies
poppy	poppies
sanctuary	sanctuaries
difficulty	difficulties

Ways to form plurals

Words that end in -f or -fe

When singular words end in -f or -fe, add -s to form the plural.

Singular	Plural
handkerchief	handkerchiefs
ruff	ruffs
roof	roofs
giraffe	giraffes
carafe	carafes
café	cafés

There are a few exceptions to this rule, where you change the f to a v and add -es for the plural.

Singular	Plural
calf	calves
elf	elves
half	halves
knife	knives
leaf	leaves
life	lives
loaf	loaves
self	selves
sheaf	sheaves
shelf	shelves
thief	thieves
wife	wives
wolf	wolves

Finally, there are a few words which may take either form

Singular	Plural
hoof	hooves OR hoofs
scarf	scarves OR scarfs
turf	turves OR turfs
wharf	wharves OR wharfs

Words that end in -o

When singular words end in -o, you usually just add -s for the plural.

Singular	Plural
avocado	avocados
banjo	banjos
pimiento	pimientos
solo	solos
studio	studios
photo	photos
verso	versos
video	videos

However, there are a few exceptions here too. These words take -es for the plural.

Singular	Plural
domino	dominoes
echo	echoes
embargo	embargoes
hero	heroes

mosquito	mosquitoes
no	noes
potato	potatoes
tomato	tomatoes
torpedo	torpedoes
veto	vetoes
volcano	volcanoes

And yet again, there are a few that take either form.

Singular	Plural
cargo	cargoes OR cargos
mango	mangoes OR mangos
memento	mementoes OR mementos

Foreign words

English contains many words that we have taken from other languages. Many of these have been absorbed fully into English and follow English grammar rules, but others have retained the rules of their original language.

Latin words ending in -a

Words taken from Latin that end in *-a* in the singular become plural by adding an *e* (the ending, *-ae,* is pronounced 'ee'). Many of these may also be seen with an English plural ending, formed by adding an *s.* Where this is common, I have given both forms.

Singular	Plural
alga	algae
alumna	alumnae
amoeba	amoebae/amoebas
antenna	antennae (of creatures)/ antennas (aerials)
formula	formulae/formulas
larva	larvae
nebula	nebulae/nebulas
pupa	pupae
vertebra	vertebrae

Latin words ending in -um

Latin words that end in *-um* change the ending to *-a* in the plural. As before, there are occasional exceptions where the English plural form is used, simply adding *-s* to the *-um*.

Singular	Plural
addendum	addenda
aquarium	aquaria/aquariums
bacterium	bacteria
curriculum	curricula
datum	data
erratum	errata
mausoleum	mausolea/mausoleums
maximum	maxima/maximums
medium	media/mediums

memorandum	memoranda/memorandums
millennium	millennia/millenniums
minimum	minima/minimums
optimum	optima/optimums
phylum	phyla
referendum	referenda/referendums
stratum	strata
ultimatum	ultimata/ultimatums
ovum	ova

> ⚠ **Watch out for *strata***
>
> It is quite common to hear people talking about *the strata of society*. *Strata* is actually the **plural** form of the Latin word *stratum,* meaning a layer. So make sure you're talking about the many layers if you use *strata*. If you are talking about just one, use *stratum*.

Latin words ending in -us

Singular Latin words ending in *-us* change to *-i* in the plural. In some cases, the English plural ending *-es* can be added instead.

Singular	Plural
alumnus	alumni
bacillus	bacilli
cactus	cacti/cactuses
focus	foci/focuses
fungus	fungi/funguses

genius	genii/geniuses
hippopotamus	hippopotami/
	hippopotamuses
nucleus	nuclei
radius	radii/radiuses
stimulus	stimuli
stylus	styli/styluses
syllabus	syllabi/syllabuses
terminus	termini/terminuses
tumulus	tumuli
villus	villi

⚠ **Watch out for exceptions in Latin!**

Even Latin has the odd exceptions to its rules: *viscus* (meaning an internal organ) takes the plural form *viscera*, which is how we usually use it in English. Similarly, *opus* (meaning a work of art) takes the plural form *opera*, which we use to mean a particular form of musical performance. But we also use the English plural form *opuses* to mean works of art.

Latin words ending in -ix

Latin words ending in *-ix* change the ending to *-ices* to form the plural. Alternatively, you can add the English plural ending *-es* to the whole word.

Singular	Plural
appendix	appendices/appendixes
index	indices (especially in technical contexts)/indexes
matrix	matrices/matrixes
vertex	vertices/vertexes
vortex	vortices/vortexes

French words ending in -u

English has acquired several French words ending in *-u* in the singular. For the plural form, most keep to the original French rules and add *-x,* although some can be anglicised and simply add *-s.*

Singular	Plural
adieu	adieux/adieus
bureau	bureaux/bureaus
chateau	chateaux
milieu	milieux/milieus
plateau	plateaux/plateaus
tableau	tableaux

Italian words ending in -o

There are a few Italian words ending in *-o* that are used in English. You will find many of these in a musical context. To form the plural, follow the Italian rule and change the *-o* to *-i.* Alternatively, for an anglicised form, just add *-s.*

Singular	Plural
libretto	libretti/librettos
tempo	tempi/tempos
virtuoso	virtuosi/virtuosos

⚠ Watch out for graffiti

Graffiti is the plural form of *graffito* (which is Italian for 'scratched'), so you should use it with a plural verb.

*The graffiti in the underpass **are** very offensive.*

Nowadays, the word is frequently used as a collective noun, referring to the writing of inscriptions in general. In this case, treat it as singular.

*Graffiti **is** becoming a serious problem in our town.*

Greek words ending in -on

These always change to *-a* in the plural, although in English usage some keep the *-on* and add *-s*.

Singular	Plural
automaton	automata/automatons
criterion	criteria
ganglion	ganglia/ganglions
phenomenon	phenomena

> ⚠ **Watch out for *criterion* and *phenomenon***
> These two are never anglicised and so they cause many
> mistakes, with the plural – *criteria* and *phenomena* – often
> being mistaken for the singular. Remember,
>> The most important criteria **are**...
>> These extraordinary phenomena **were**...

Words that don't change

Some singular words are the same in the singular and the plural
form.

aircraft	bison
cannon	deer
dozen*	fish
grouse	sheep
shot (bullets)	swine

*Dozens of is often used colloquially to mean *lots of* – but it is
not strictly correct.

> ⚠ **Look out for *fish***
> As well as the word *fish* itself, most types of fish adhere to
> the 'no change' rule: *bream, cod, haddock, salmon, sole,
> trout, herring,* etc. However, small fish – such as *pilchards,
> sardines* and *sprats* – take the usual *-s* in the plural form
> *Fish* may also be used in the plural form *fishes*.

A few nouns are never used in the singular.

barracks
bellows
billiards
gallows
measles
news
pincers
pliers
scissors
shears
spectacles
thanks
tidings
tongs
trousers
tweezers
victuals

There are exceptions when the noun is being used attributively – that is, attributed, or attached, to another noun in a descriptive way:

billiard ball
trouser press
trouser leg
pincer movement

Plurals of hyphenated words

When forming plurals of hyphenated words, make sure you add the *s* to the right part. Try to think what it is that is increasing in number. In most cases, it is the first word that you should change.

Singular	Plural
brother-in-law	brothers-in-law
sister-in-law	sisters-in-law
mother-in-law	mothers-in-law
father-in-law	fathers-in-law
daughter-in-law	daughters-in-law
son-in-law	sons-in-law
coat-of-arms	coats-of-arms
hanger-on	hangers-on
maid-of-honour	maids-of-honour
man-of-war	men-of-war
passer-by	passers-by

In the following examples, however, it is clearly the second word that is being increased in number, so that one takes the *s*.

Singular	Plural
bye-law	bye-laws
do-gooder	do-gooders
mouse-trap	mouse-traps
man-eater	man-eaters

Irregular plurals

Some words have strange plurals that you just have to learn!

Singular	Plural
brother (in a religious context)	brethren
child	children
die	dice
foot	feet
goose	geese
louse	lice
man	men
mouse	mice
ox	oxen
person	people
tooth	teeth
woman	women

⚠ **Watch out for *mongoose***
The plural of *mongoose* is *mongooses* – not *mongeese*.

Chapter 4
Confusing Words

There are many pairs (or even larger groups) of words in the English language that sound similar but don't mean the same thing. There are also words that sound quite different yet have similar meanings. In this chapter, I have listed the words that most commonly cause confusion, so that you can check which one you should use and when. There is also more information in Words that Sound the Same, starting on page 152.

Accede/exceed
To accede means *to agree to*.

> The police refused to accede to the demands of the kidnappers.

It can also mean *to take office*, especially of a king or queen.

> Prince Charles will accede to the throne when Queen Elizabeth II dies or abdicates.

To exceed means *to go beyond, to surpass*.

> It is very easy to exceed the speed limit, especially if you don't know the road.

Accept/except

To accept means *to give an affirmative answer to.*

> We accept your invitation with great pleasure.

It can also mean *to tolerate* or *to submit to.*

> He accepted the umpire's decision.

> The children accepted their new stepmother.

Except is a preposition that means *other than.*

> All our friends were there except Bob and Alice.

Adverse/averse

Adverse means *unfavourable.*

> The adverse weather spoilt their holiday.

Averse means *opposed (to).*

> I am not averse to the odd glass of sherry!

Advice/advise

Advice means *recommendation.*

> The doctor's advice was that he should rest.

To advise is the verbal form of the same word, meaning *to recommend.*

> I advise you to think it over.

Affect/effect

To affect usually means *to have an impact on.*

> The fall in the stock market will *affect* share prices.

It can also mean *to put on* or *to pretend.*

> She *affected* indifference at his proposition.

Affected is an adjective, meaning *put on, artificial.*

> Everyone loathed her *affected* manner.

To effect means *to bring about.*

> The punishment has *effected* a change for the better in his behaviour.

Effect may also be used as a noun, meaning a *consequence* or *result.*

> The strike had the desired *effect.*

It can also mean *the state of being operative.*

> The new law comes into *effect* from next July.

A third meaning is *an impression made upon a spectator.*

> She gazed in the mirror, thrilled with the *effect* of her new outfit.

Effects (plural) means *the lighting, sound, etc. in a film or play.*

> The film's special *effects* were terrifyingly realistic.

It can also mean *belongings.*

> Please take all your personal *effects* with you when you leave the aircraft.

Affective/effective

Affective means *emotional, concerning the affections.*

> Last night's television programme about reuniting broken families was deeply *affective* and reduced all of us to tears.

Effective means *having the desired result.*

> Aspirin is an *effective* cure for headaches.

All together/altogether
All together means *all in one place or time.*
> The children came into the kitchen all together.

Altogether means *in total* or *overall.*
> It had been a very successful day altogether.
> Altogether, there were twenty children in the class.

Allude/elude
To allude means *to refer to something indirectly.*
> Jane's husband never missed an opportunity to allude to her criminal past, dropping little hints into every conversation.

To elude means *to escape.*
> The fox eluded the hounds by wading across the river to conceal its scent.
> I am puzzled by her extraordinary behaviour. The reason for it eludes me.

Allusion/delusion/illusion
An allusion is *an indirect reference, a hint.*
> In her speech, she made an allusion to the plot to remove her from the board of directors.

A delusion is *a mistaken idea.*
> His delusion that he could control the situation was shattered when the argument broke out.

An illusion is *a deceptive appearance.*
> The magician completed the illusion by apparently sawing the lady in half.

It can also mean *a mistaken idea*.

> A mirage is an optical illusion.
> He was under the illusion that he could fly.

Allusive/elusive
Allusive means *hinting at*.

> She spoke about her new relationship in an allusive way,
> dropping occasional hints about another man.

Elusive means *difficult to catch or recall*.

> The elusive butterfly fluttered all round the garden, just out
> of reach.
> The truth of the matter proved to be elusive; no one would
> answer her questions.

Alternate/alternative
Alternate means *every other*.

> We go shopping on alternate Fridays.

To alternate means *to change repeatedly between two conditions*.

> I alternate between loving and hating TV soap operas.

An alternative is *one of two choices*.

> The alternative to going by train would be to go by car.

However, nowadays it is often used (incorrectly) to mean one of
any number of options.

> There are several alternatives – we could go by car, coach,
> train or plane.

A better alternative would be to use the word *choices*!

Ambiguous/ambivalent

Ambiguous means *giving two meanings.*

> The ambiguous letter from the solicitors caused a heated argument over what it actually meant.

Ambivalent means *experiencing conflicting emotions at the same time.*

> The victim had ambivalent feelings towards the pathetic urchin who stole her purse.

Amiable/amicable

Amiable means *likeable and friendly.*

> My old spaniel was the most amiable dog imaginable. He wouldn't hurt a fly.

Amicable means *done in a friendly way.*

> They settled their differences in an amicable way that left both feeling satisfied.

Among/between

Both these words are used with the word *share*. The choice depends on how many are sharing.

Among should be used when three or more people or things share something.

> We shared the bag of sweets among the six children.

Between should be used if an item is to be shared by just two people or things.

> We divided the cake between the two plates.

Between may also be used to indicate a point relative to two or more others in space or time, or in relationships.

> There is no love lost between the Blakes and the Smiths.
>
> France is situated between Spain, Belgium, Switzerland and Germany.
>
> They arrived between two and three o'clock.

Amoral/immoral

These are subtly different.

Amoral means *having no moral standards*. An amoral person lacks morals in the sense that he does not appreciate or even understand right from wrong. He stands outside moral laws.

Immoral means *corrupt* or *promiscuous*. An immoral person knows right from wrong and chooses the latter. He knowingly breaks moral laws.

Anathema/enigma

Anathema means *a detestable person or thing*. It is used without the indefinite article (*an*).

> The wicked murderer was anathema to the young detective.

An enigma is *a puzzle*.

> The workings of the murderer's mind were a total enigma to the detective.

Anticipate/expect
To anticipate means *to be aware of something in advance and act accordingly.*

> The residents anticipated the flood, piling sand bags up against their doors.

To expect means *to assume something will follow in the future.*

> The residents expected the river to burst its banks at high tide.
> I expect you to arrive on time every morning.

Arbitrate/mediate
To arbitrate means *to settle a dispute.* It is used of a judge or other authoritative party.

> The judge who arbitrated in the dispute ruled that the management should give a 4 per cent pay rise to the staff.

To mediate means *to intervene in a dispute to bring about peace.*

> The twins' mother often had to mediate in their arguments over toys. She always succeeded in persuading them to share.

As if/as though/like
All these expressions are used when making comparisons.

As if/as though may be used to precede a clause in expressions such as *look as if* and *feel as though,* etc., when making a comparison to a situation. Do not use **like** in this way.

> She looked as if/as though she had been dragged through a hedge backwards.
> His face reddened like he had been slapped. ✗

91

Like should only be used with a noun, when drawing a comparison to a person or thing.

> *He tried to behave like his father.*
>
> *The bird dropped like a stone on to its prey.*

Assume/presume

To assume means *to accept as true, without proof or reason.*

> *I assume you take milk in your tea.*
>
> *You should not assume that life will always be the same.*

To presume means *to believe something, based on available evidence.*

> *I presumed that, as they had met before, they would remember each other's names.*

Assurance/insurance

Assurance means *certainty* or *guarantee.*

> *At the post office, she sought assurance that the parcel would be delivered the next day.*

It is very often used in a technical sense to mean insurance, as in *life assurance policy,* when a pay-out is guaranteed in the event of an inevitable occurrence, usually death.

> *A life assurance policy is a sensible way of saving money for your family's future.*

Insurance means *protection against risk.* The event insured – such as accident, theft, illness etc. – may never happen, so there is no guarantee involved.

We take out travel insurance every year, but we have never had to make a claim.

Assure/ensure/insure

To assure means *to say with confidence (that something will happen).*

I assure you I will be home by midnight.

To ensure means *to make certain (that something will happen).*

By taking the proper precautions, they ensured their safety.

To insure means *to protect against financial risk.*

We've even insured the dog against illness.

Astrology/astronomy

Astrology means *the study of the movement of the stars, interpreted as an influence on people's lives.*

I always read the astrology charts in magazines.

Astronomy means *the scientific study of the stars.*

The only thing I know about astronomy is that the earth revolves around the sun.

Authorised/authoritative

Authorised means *officially approved.*

The committee was authorised to make the necessary repairs to the clubhouse.

Authoritative means *convincing, being recognised as an authority, self-confident.*

The teacher had an authoritative air when she addressed the class.

Autobiography/biography
Autobiography means *one's own life story.*
Biography means *the life story of another person.*

Avenge/revenge
To avenge means *to seek revenge or retribution.*
The young earl avenged the death of his father by killing the murderer's entire family.
Revenge means *(act of or desire for) retaliation, getting one's own back.*
Jimmy got his revenge by hiding a frog in the bully's rucksack.

Averse *see* Adverse

Avoid/evade
These mean the same. However, it is worth pointing out that *tax avoidance* is not such a great crime as *tax evasion* (the latter suggests some kind of deliberate subterfuge).

Bath/bathe
A bath is *a container in which you sit or lie to wash yourself.*
She filled the bath with hot, sudsy water.
To bath means *to wash (something or someone)* in a bath.

To bathe means *to cleanse (a wound)*

> She went upstairs to bathe the cuts on her arms in cool water.

It may also mean *to swim*.

> The water was warm so he decided to bathe in the sea.

A bathe is *the act of swimming*.

> The water was warm so he decided to go for a bathe in the sea.

Beside/besides

Beside means *next to*.

> I put a glass of water beside my bed.

Besides means *in addition to*.

> Besides being a trombone player, Mary is also a singer.

Between *see* Among

Biannual/biennial

Biannual means *occurring twice a year*.

> We have biannual conferences, held in May and October.

Biennial means *occurring once every two years or lasting for two years*.

> The biennial conference was held in 2000 and 2002.

Borrow/lend

To borrow *means to have temporary use of something belonging to another person*.

> I can borrow my mother's car.

To lend means *to allow someone temporary use of your belongings.*

> My mother will lend me her car.

Never use either word as a noun.

> Give me a lend/a borrow of your car.   ✗

Both/each/either

Both means *each of two.*

> Brush the meat with oil on both sides.

Each means *every one of two or more.*

> Brush each slice of meat with oil.

Either means *one or the other.*

> I don't mind if I have the meat or the fish – either will do.

It may also be used to mean *both.*

> Her hair was tied up in pigtails on either side of her head.

This may cause confusion, as in the following example:

> Brush oil on either side of the chop.   ✗

It is not clear whether one is to oil one or both sides of the chop. In such a case, use *both.*

> Brush oil on both sides of the chop.   ✔

Bought/brought

Bought is the past tense of the verb *to buy.*

> I bought a bar of chocolate at the shop.

Brought is the past tense of the verb *to bring.*

> I brought three friends with me to the party.

Breath/breathe

Breath is a noun. It refers to the air that is taken in or exhaled from the lungs.

He took a deep breath before diving into the water.

To breathe is *the action of inhaling or exhaling air.*

He had to breathe deeply to regain his composure.

Can/may

I can means *I am able.*

I can ride my bike now that my broken leg has healed.

I may means *I am permitted.*

Mum says I may ride my bike down to the shops.

Nowadays, however, **can** tends to be used in either context.

Censor/censure

To censor means *to suppress material that is unsuitable for publication* (particularly of TV and films).

The film was censored because it contained too much bad language.

Used as a noun, it also refers to the person who does the checking.

The censor gave the film an 18 rating because of its explicit sex scenes.

To censure means *to criticise harshly.*

The chairman of the company was censured for his underhand share dealing.

Capital/corporal (punishment)

Capital refers to the head. Therefore **capital punishment** means punishment by injury to the head, in other words execution by some means.

Corporal refers to the body. Therefore **corporal punishment** involves punishment by injury to the body, usually beating.

Centenarian/centurion

A **centenarian** is a person who is at least 100 years old.

A **centurion** is a Roman army commander, leading 100 men.

Ceremonial/ceremonious

Ceremonial may be used as an adjective to describe the rituals associated with formal public or religious events.

> *The priest donned his ceremonial vestments, ready for the royal wedding.*

As a noun, it refers to the rituals themselves.

> *The children watching the ritual were fascinated by the elaborate ceremonial.*

Ceremonious is an adjective used to describe an elaborate ritual, or a person who shows a particular fondness for formality and ritual.

> *The royal wedding was a truly ceremonious affair, lasting for several hours.*

> *Despite his inexperience, the young priest conducted the whole event in a duly dignified, ceremonious manner.*

Childish/childlike
Childish means *immature*. It implies silliness.

> Stop being so childish and act your age!

Childlike means *like a child*. It implies purity and innocence.

> Her petite figure and big blue eyes gave her an almost
> childlike appearance.

Climatic/climactic
Climatic relates to the climate.

> Climatic changes are affecting all parts of the world.

Climactic relates to a climax.

> The climactic moment in the film came when the car
> plunged over the cliff.

Clothes/cloths
Clothes are garments.

> She packed her clothes into the suitcase.

Cloths are pieces of material used for cleaning.

> The man picked up the cloths and began washing the car.

Coherent/cohesive
Coherent means forming a logical argument.

> The lawyer made a very coherent speech when summing up
> for the jury.

Cohesive means unified.

> Every sports coach works towards building a cohesive team.

Common/mutual

Common can be used to mean *ordinary*.

> The common people knew little of the life of the royal family.

It may also mean *belonging to* or *shared or done by more than one person*.

> It is common knowledge that the woman down the road is having an affair with the milkman.

Mutual also means *shared* but it refers to reciprocal feelings or actions between two or more people.

> Their mutual admiration was immense. He regarded her as the most beautiful girl in the world. She believed he was the wittiest man that ever lived.

Many people use the phrase *our mutual friend* to refer to a shared friend but, in fact, *our common friend* is correct – although obviously open to misinterpretation!

Compelling/compulsive/compulsory

Compelling means *forceful* or *arousing strong interest or attention*.

> The young doctor was very popular amongst his patients. Young women in particular quickly fell under the spell of his compelling personality.

Compulsive means *obsessive*.

> The man confessed that he never told the truth – he was a compulsive liar.

They may both be used of an experience, for instance a book or a film, to mean something that grips the attention.

The book was a compelling/compulsive read.

The film made compelling/compulsive viewing.

Compulsory means *required by a rule or law.*

Mathematics, English and science are all compulsory and must be studied by every child.

Compliment/Complement

Compliment means *an expression of praise.* It may be used as a verb in the same way.

He was always paying her compliments, admiring her hair and her choice of clothes.

He complimented her on her appearance.

Complement means *something that completes.* It is often used in the expression *the full complement,* meaning the full number.

The full complement of the ship's crew was required to be on duty on the first day of the cruise.

It may also be used as a verb, to mean *to complete* or *go together as a pair.*

Her jewellery complemented her dress.

Compose/comprise/consist

These all mean *is made up of.* They are all used in slightly different ways.

An orange is **composed of** several segments.

An orange **consists of** several segments.

An orange **comprises** several segments.

> ### ⚠ Watch out for *comprise*
> **Comprise** is a transitive verb (see page 10), and should never be preceded by *is, was,* etc., or followed by the word *of.* The following sentence is therefore wrong on two counts.
>
> > The meal was comprised of three courses.　　　　✗
>
> To help you avoid making these mistakes, think of it as meaning *contain.*

Comprehensible/comprehensive
Comprehensible means *understandable.*

> Although the film was in French, the subtitles made it comprehensible to the English audience.

Comprehensive means *including all aspects.*

> Before I went on holiday to Spain, I bought a comprehensive guide to the country.

Concave/convex
Concave describes *something that curves inwards* (think of 'caves in' to make it easy to remember).

> There was a concave impression in the soft earth, where a cannonball had landed.

Convex describes **something that curves outwards.**

> Slowly a convex swelling appeared on his forehead.

Contagious/infectious

Both refer to diseases and how they are passed on.

Contagious describes a disease transferred by direct bodily contact, such as AIDS.

Infectious describes a disease carried in the air or by water, such as the common cold.

You can use either adjective in a figurative sense.

A wave of infectious laughter spread round the table.

Contemptible/contemptuous

Both adjectives come from the noun *contempt*.

Contemptible means *liable to or deserving of contempt*.

The bully constantly taunted smaller, weaker boys. His behaviour was contemptible.

Contemptuous means *full of contempt*.

The boy was contemptuous of the school's rules forbidding bullying and constantly taunted smaller, weaker boys.

Continual/continuous

Continual means *occurring frequently but intermittently*. It implies that the action goes on happening but is broken every now and then.

Throughout the summer, the police made continual speed checks on vehicles driving past the school.

Continuous means *incessant*. There are no breaks in the action.

The continuous droning of the engines was almost deafening.

Council/counsel

Council is a noun, meaning *an administrative group, an assembly of advisers.*

> The parish council meets twice a month to discuss local issues.

A councillor is *someone elected to sit on a council.*

Counsel as a noun is used to mean *advice,* usually given by a person in authority.

> The young warrior sought counsel from the elders of the tribe as to how to approach the chief for the hand of his daughter in marriage.
>
> I took counsel from a barrister before deciding to sue my former employers.

It may also be used as a verb, particularly in the sense of giving advice on personal or emotional problems.

> After the accident a team was sent to counsel the victims.

A counsellor is a person who gives advice in this way.

> As a professional counsellor, she spent a large proportion of her time listening to other people's problems.

Credible/creditable/credulous

Credible means *plausible* or *believable.*

> The boy's version of the events leading up to the robbery was clear and credible. His story was believed by the police.

Creditable means *deserving credit* or *praiseworthy.*

> The young musician's creditable performance on the piano made him a strong contender for the prize.

Credulous means *gullible* or *too ready to believe.*

> The credulous old man let the stranger into his house, entirely believing her claim that she was from Social Services.

Deceitful/deceptive

Deceitful means *deliberately dishonest.*

> As a child, his behaviour was frequently deceitful. He regularly stole money from his mother and lied constantly.

Deceptive means *apt to mislead.*

> His appearance was deceptive. Behind that innocent little face lurked a cold, calculating brain.
>
> The sky was deceptively cloudy and, not realising the strength of the sun, we all got badly burned.

Decided/decisive

These adjectives can both mean *firm.*

> The mayor was of the decided opinion that action had to be taken immediately.
>
> Faced with an emergency, the authorities took immediate and decisive action.

Decided also means *perceptible, clear.*

> There was a decided quiver in her voice when she spoke of her lost pet.

Decisive also means *conclusive.*

> The evidence was decisive and the burglar was convicted.

Defective/deficient
Defective means *faulty*.

> The defective light bulb flickered on and off.

Deficient means *incomplete* or *lacking a vital component*.

> Children who are deficient in vitamin D may suffer from a disease called rickets.

Definite/definitive
Definite means *exact* or *sure*.

> My father's answer was quite definite. There was no misunderstanding him.

Definitive means *unconditional* or *final*.

> My father's answer, a definitive 'no', made it clear that argument was useless. His decision was final and would never be changed.

Delusion *see* Allusion

Deride/derive
To deride is *to pour scorn on*.

> John derided Mary for her rather silly ideas.

To derive is *to obtain from*.

> John derived pleasure from jeering at Mary's ideas.

Derisive/derisory
Derisive means *unpleasantly scornful.*
> His derisive remarks caused some offence.

Derisory means *so insignificant as to be worthy of scorn.*
> The trade union turned down the management's offer, declaring it to be derisory, and the strike continued.

Desert/dessert
Desert means *an arid wilderness.*
> Camels can survive in the desert for many days without water.

Dessert means *a sweet course at the end of a meal.*
> We all picked our puddings from the dessert trolley.

> ⚠ Watch our for *your just deserts*
> The phrase *to get your just deserts* means to get your come-uppance. Many people think it is *to get your just desserts* (which would be something to do with puddings and is entirely wrong!).

Diagnosis/prognosis
Diagnosis is *identification of an illness or problem through examination of the symptoms.*
> The doctor examined the child thoroughly and then made his diagnosis – typhoid.

Prognosis is *predicted outcome.*
> The prognosis was not good. He did not think she would recover.

⚠ **Watch out for *dinghy* and *dingy***

This pair of words have very different meanings. The pronunciation should give you a clue to the different spellings.

A **dinghy** is *a small boat*.

> They climbed into the dinghy and rowed across the lake.

Dingy means *grimy*.

> The squat was dark and dingy inside.

Discover/invent

To discover means *to find/become aware of something that already exists*.

> Christopher Columbus discovered America.

To invent means *to create or devise for the first time*.

> In 1764, James Hargreaves invented the Spinning Jenny.

It is correct, therefore, to say

> James Watt's discovery of the power of steam led to the invention of steam engines.

Disinterested/uninterested

Disinterested means *impartial, having no self-interest*. It does **not** mean *having no interest*, or *bored by*.

> Since I was not involved in the dispute, I was able to offer disinterested advice to the couple.

Uninterested means *bored by or with.*

> Her boyfriend was totally uninterested in her purchases and hardly bothered to suppress a yawn as she laid them out.

Displaced/misplaced

Displaced means *exiled* or *moved from its proper place.*

> We have a large number of displaced persons in the hostel, mainly refugees from the war in the East.

Misplaced means *lost* or *put in the wrong place.*

> I've misplaced my car keys again.

Distinct/distinctive

Distinct means *unmistakable* or *clear.*

> The old man walked with a distinct limp.

Distinctive means *individually characteristic.*

> The radio news presenter had a distinctive, deep voice.

Distinguished/distinguishing

Distinguished means *eminent, of high standing.*

> I am pleased to welcome a most distinguished guest to our dinner tonight.

Distinguishing means *making it different from the rest.*

> The distinguishing characteristic of the final contestant was the clarity of her performance. Unlike the others, she could be heard at the back of the room.

Dominating/dominant/domineering

Dominating means *exercising control over.*

> During the holiday, Peter's dominating attitude became very irritating as he tried to control everything the group did.

Dominant means *most influential.*

> The dominant male lion protected the females in the pride from the attentions of younger males.

Domineering means *arrogant and overbearing.*

> His domineering wife bullied him constantly and would never let him do or say anything without her say-so.

Down to/up to

Both of these expressions are concerned with responsibility.

Down to means *due to* or *the responsibility of.*

> The success of the garden party was down to the beautiful weather.

> We put her absence down to illness.

Up to means *incumbent on,* when offering a choice of accepting responsibility.

> It's up to you whether we go to the cinema or not.

Due to/owing to

These are not interchangeable.

Due to means *the result of* and should be used when referring to a noun. Do not use it as a substitute for *because of.*

> His lateness was due to an accident.

Owing to means *because of* and should be used when referring to a verb.

> He was late owing to an accident.

Eatable/edible

Eatable means *able to be eaten.* The food can be consumed although it may not be appetising.

> The apples were eatable even though they were not quite ripe.

Edible means *safe to eat.*

> Are you sure that the mushrooms you picked are edible?
> Sheep's eyes are edible but very few people in the West find them eatable.

Eclipse/ellipse

To eclipse means *to put in the shade.* It may be used literally, as in

> The moon eclipsed the sun

and figuratively, as in

> Her beauty eclipsed that of all the other ladies in the room.

Eclipse may also be used as a noun.

> During the eclipse of the sun, the sky darkened and the temperature dropped.

Ellipse is a *geometrical term,* meaning a regular oval shape. You are more likely to use the adjective elliptical.

> The elliptical shape of a rugby ball differentiates it from those used in other sports.

Effect *see* **Affect**

Effective/effectual
Effective means *having the desired result.*

> Peppermint tea is an effective cure for heartburn.

Effectual means *capable of producing the desired result.*

> Making notes is an effectual way of remembering details.

Egoist/egotist
These are very similar.

An egoist is someone who selfishly puts himself first, never thinking of others.

An egotist is someone who thinks a lot of himself and assumes everyone else does too!

Either ... or/neither ... nor
Use **either** followed by **or.**

> Either you or I must go and buy the tickets.
>
> You can only have one treat: either a trip to the cinema or a day at the zoo.

Note that **either ... or** implies a choice between **only two** things. The following example is wrong.

> You can cook the fish either in the oven or on the hob or in a
> microwave.   ✗

Neither must always be followed by **nor.** They are always used in a negative sense.

> Neither you nor I can go out this evening.

They may be used about any number of people or things.

> Neither the cat, the dog nor the rabbits have eaten much
> today because it is so hot.

Note the use of the plural verb in the last example. The verb has to agree with the nearest noun, so if the noun is singular, it takes the corresponding singular form of the verb; if the noun is plural, it takes the corresponding plural form.

Elder/older

Older is *the comparative form of old.*

> My dog is older than yours.
>
> The older boys play in a separate part of the grounds.

Elder is used only when comparing the ages of two people, to mean *of greater age* or *senior.* (There is no such adjective as *eld*!)

> My elder sister, Lisa, was much prettier than my younger
> sister, Bella.

Elders, the plural term, is used to refer to *people of greater age and seniority.*

> You should respect your elders and betters.

Eligible/illegible

Eligible means *entitled to be chosen.*

> The constable was eligible for promotion to sergeant.

Illegible means *impossible to read.*

> The girl lost marks in her exam because her handwriting
> was illegible.

Elude *see* **Allude**

Elusive *see* **Allusive**

Emigrate/immigrate

To **emigrate** means *to leave one's home country*. It is always followed by *from*.

We are going to emigrate from England to Canada.

To **immigrate** means *to enter as a permanent resident in a country other than one's own*. It is always followed by *to*.

People from many different nationalities immigrate to the UK every year.

Eminent/imminent

Eminent means *distinguished*.

The retired eminent opera diva, Lady Violet Bountiful, was welcomed enthusiastically as a member of the Music Society.

Imminent means *impending*.

The birth of Mary's baby was imminent so Joseph tried to find them a bed for the night.

Empathise/sympathise

To **empathise** means *to identify with and understand feelings as a result of shared experience*.

Having spent several months in a wheelchair, I can really empathise with permanently disabled people.

To sympathise means *to share feelings with.*

> I sympathised with my friend's evident bitterness at the injustice done to her.

Endemic/epidemic

Epidemic as a noun means *a widespread outbreak* (usually of disease).

> If people don't have their children vaccinated, we could soon see an epidemic of measles.

It may be also be used as an adjective.

> At first there were only a few isolated cases of measles amongst the children, but within weeks the outbreak had reached epidemic proportions, with people of all ages being affected.

Endemic has much the same meanings, both as noun and adjective, but refers to disease etc. in a specific area or group.

> The African AIDS endemic is almost out of control.
> Smoking cannabis seems to be endemic among young people today.

Enigma *see* **Anathema**

Ensure *see* **Assure**

Envious/jealous
Envious means *feeling discontented due to someone else's good fortune*.

> I am so envious of my friends who are going to Australia.

Jealous is stronger and means *resentful*.

> I was deeply jealous of my sister who had recently learned to drive. It seemed unfair that I still had to go everywhere by bus.

Used in the adverbial form, it means *in a fiercely protective way*.

> The swan jealously guarded her nest against any predators.

Epigram/epitaph/epithet
An epigram is *a witty saying*.

> Work is the curse of the drinking classes.

An epitaph is *an inscription on a tombstone* or *other words written about someone who has died*.

> Here lies Fred who was alive and now is dead.

An epithet is *a nickname*, describing a quality of the person.

> Wellington was known as the Iron Duke because of his firm, disciplined personality and attitudes.

Equable/equitable
Equable means *calm, composed*.

> My grandmother had such an equable disposition that she never raised her voice.

Equitable means *fair, impartial*.

> The parties came to an equitable agreement that suited everyone.

Especially/specially
Especially means *exceptionally*.
> I had an especially good time at the nightclub.

Specially is less intense, meaning *particularly*.
> You have been specially chosen to receive a prize.

Exalted/exulted/exultant
Exalted is an adjective meaning *high-ranking*.
> The prince's exalted position meant that he never really understood ordinary people.

Exulted is the past participle of the verb *to exult*, which means *to rejoice*.
> The warriors exulted in the success of their campaign against the neighbouring tribe.

Exultant means *overjoyed*.
> The family were exultant when they heard they'd won the holiday competition.

Except *see* Accept

Exhausting/exhaustive
Exhausting means *extremely tiring*.
> At the end of an exhausting day, it's good to sit in a warm bath and relax.

Exhaustive means *comprehensive*.
> The police made an exhaustive search of the premises.

Exhort/extort

To exhort means *to urge on*.

> The coach exhorted his team to ever greater efforts throughout the match.

To extort means *to remove by force*.

> The villain extorted money from his victim by threatening to break his legs.

Expect *see* Anticipate

Explicit/implicit

Explicit means *clear*.

> He gave me explicit directions on how to reach the venue. Unfortunately, they turned out to be incorrect.

Implicit means *implied but not outwardly expressed*.

> His implicit remarks caused them to doubt his integrity.

It can also mean *unquestioning*.

> I have implicit faith in your abilities.

Famous/infamous

Famous means *well-known*.

> The Beatles is one of the most famous pop groups of all time.

Infamous means *well-known for something unpleasant*.

> Jack the Ripper was infamous for the series of horrible crimes he committed.

> ⚠ **Watch out for *notorious***
> *Notorious* can be used instead of *infamous,* but it may also be used in less sinister contexts where *infamous* would not be appropriate.
> John was notorious for getting drunk on a Friday night.

Fewer/less

Fewer is the comparative form of *few* and means *not so many.* Use **fewer** when referring to numbers of people or things, i.e. things that may be counted individually.

> There were fewer people in the restaurant today than there were yesterday.
> We served fewer than fifty dinners.

Less is the comparative form of *little* and means *not so much.* Use **less** when referring to an amount of something that you are quantifying as a whole. **Less than** is used with quantity, time and distance.

> You should put less sugar in your tea.
> I have less money in my purse than I thought.
> It is less than three minutes until the train comes.
> It is less than six miles to the next town.

See also Comparative and Superlative Adjectives, page 31.

Fictional/fictitious
Fictional means *related to or derived from fiction*.

All the characters in the book were fictional.

Fictitious means *invented*.

She gave a fictitious name to the police.

Flammable/inflammable/non-flammable
Flammable means *easily set on fire*. It is commonly used in America.

Nightwear made of flammable material is a potential fire hazard.

Inflammable means exactly the same and is the English version of the word.

The sofa carried a warning label that the stuffing was inflammable.

Note that it is **not** the opposite of *flammable* and because of the obvious potential for confusion, *flammable* is now more widely used.

Non-flammable is the opposite of both **flammable** and **inflammable,** meaning *not easily set on fire*.

For safety, children's clothes should always be made of non-flammable materials.

Flaunt/flout
To flaunt means *to show off*.

Prostitutes flaunt themselves at the side of the road.

To flout means *to express contempt (towards rules) through one's actions.*

> The youngsters repeatedly flouted the curfew laws, playing out in the streets until midnight.

Flounder/founder
To flounder means *to struggle, as though in mud.*

> The drowning man floundered helplessly in the waves.

To founder means *to sink* or *fall down.*

> The tanker foundered on the rocks, spilling oil into the sea.

⚠ Watch out for *forest* and *wood*

These nouns both refer to areas of trees. When I was young, I was told that a forest comprised all the same species; a wood was a mixture of species. More technically, in addition to this, a forest is quite dense, with 60–100 per cent tree cover, whereas a wood is more open with 25–60 per cent tree cover.

Fortuitous/fortunate
Both these words have to do with luck.

Fortuitous means *due to luck, chance or accident.*

> Peter's fortuitous meeting with the head of the BBC led to an exciting new career.

Fortunate means *lucky.*

> I am very fortunate to have a wonderful, caring family.

Gambit/gamut

A gambit is *a planned opening tactic* either in a game or in a discussion.

> He knew his gambit had paid off when the directors immediately voted him back on the board.

A gamut is *a range of something*.

> His criminal record ran the full gamut of misdemeanours from petty thieving to murder.

Gourmand/gourmet

A gourmand is a glutton, someone who is excessively fond of food.

> The fact that he was so overweight suggested that he was a gourmand.

A gourmet is a connoisseur of good food.

> The gourmet knew all the finest restaurants in the city.

Grand/grandiose

Grand means *impressive*.

> The hotel was built in the grand Victorian style, with high ceilings and elaborately decorated plasterwork.
>
> My aunt had a very grand manner, guaranteed to quell any bad behaviour amongst her nephews.

Grandiose means *extravagant, planned on an ambitious scale*.

> He was full of grandiose plans that never seemed to materialise.

Hanged/hung *see* Verbs, page 9.

Historic/historical
Historic means *important in history*.

> The Queen's Golden Jubilee was a historic occasion.

Historical means *relating to history*.

> I enjoy reading historical novels – especially those set in medieval times.

Honorary/honourable
Honorary means *given as an honour without the usual requirements*.

> Many famous people who have no academic qualifications are awarded honorary degrees from top universities.

Honourable means *worthy of honour*.

> He was an honourable man: kind, trustworthy and highly respected.

Human/humane
Human means *characteristic of a human being*. It is used particularly to indicate weakness.

> He is only human after all.

Humane means *compassionate*.

> It was agreed that the humane thing to do was to have the injured dog put to sleep.

Hyper-/hypo-

Hyper- means *excessive, going beyond or above what is normal, having too much,* as in

> Hypermarket (a huge supermarket), hypertension (abnormally high blood pressure), hyperinflation (monetary inflation at a very high rate), hypercritical (excessively critical)

Hypo- means *under, being below what is normal,* for example

> Hypodermic (going under the skin), hypo-allergenic (having a reduced tendency to cause allergies), hypoxia (having too little oxygen)

Since these prefixes change the meaning of a word in opposite ways, it is important not to confuse them. The following example illustrates this perfectly.

Hyperthermia means *having an abnormally high temperature.*

> The patient was suffering from hyperthermia so the doctor ordered that he be bathed in cool water to reduce his temperature.

Hypothermia means *having an abnormally low temperature.*

> When he was rescued from the icy water, the sailor was suffering from hypothermia. It took several hours to raise his temperature to normal.

Illusion *see* **Allusion**

Imaginary/imaginative

Imaginary means *invented.*

> Young children often have imaginary friends who seem to be very real to them.

Imaginative means *creative.*

> She is a very imaginative cook, always experimenting with different herbs and spices.

Immoral *see* Amoral

Imply/infer

To imply means *to hint at through one's own actions or words.*

> My boss implied that I would soon be out of a job.

To infer means *to draw a conclusion from someone else's actions or words.*

> I inferred from what he was saying that I should look for work elsewhere.

Impracticable/impractical

Impracticable means *impossible.*

> It was impracticable to try to move all the furniture by herself.

Impractical means *not feasible or realistic.*

> John's poor navigation skills made his plan to sail round the world wholly impractical.

Indignity/indignation
Indignity means *the state of being undignified, humiliation.*
> I hope I don't suffer the indignity of becoming incontinent.

Indignation means *righteous anger.*
> Her indignation was obvious when the police officers arrived with a warrant to search her flat.

Industrial/industrious
Industrial means *to do with industry.*
> Disposing of industrial waste is a serious problem for manufacturers.

Industrious means *hard-working.*
> Bees are industrious insects that work constantly, collecting nectar for the hive.

Ineffective/ineffectual
Ineffective means *useless, not achieving the desired result.*
> The advertising campaign was ineffective; the new brand of washing powder still didn't sell well.

Ineffectual means *lacking the ability to achieve results.* It is normally used of a person.
> The teacher was an ineffectual disciplinarian whose classes were always a riot.

Inflammable/inflammatory

Inflammable means *combustible, easily set on fire.*

> Petrol is an inflammable liquid.

Inflammatory means *tending to cause anger.*

> Her inflammatory comments immediately started an argument.

Ingenious/ingenuous/disingenuous

Ingenious means *inventive.*

> He wrote an ingenious piece of music for the concert.

Ingenuous means *innocent.*

> The child's ingenuous remarks about her grandmother's appearance caused a few people to smile.

Ingenuous can also mean *frank.*

> Her ingenuous comments were entirely honest. She had none of her sister's guile.

Disingenuous means *dishonest, having secret motives.*

> Her claim that she has no money is disingenuous, to say the least. We know that she inherited a large sum from her aunt only last year.

Inhuman/inhumane

Both mean *cruel.*

Inhuman is used of *people.*

> He was so rude and unpleasant, people thought him inhuman.

Inhumane is used to describe the *actions of inhuman people.*

> In my opinion, it is inhumane to keep battery hens.

Irony/sarcasm

Both of these involve humour of sorts.

Irony takes a wry view of events. Its humour involves a subtle appreciation of the paradoxical nature of a situation. It draws a contrast between what might be expected and what actually happens.

> It was deeply ironic that the only person to drown in the boating accident was a one-time international swimming star.
>
> The full irony of the situation struck him when he realised that because of the damage the floods had caused to the mains water pipes, there was no water to drink.

Sarcasm has been called the lowest form of wit. It is more direct and unpleasant than irony and relies entirely on the tone of voice used. Apparently harmless or even complimentary words are spoken in such a way as to cause hurt. Imagine the following said with a slight sneer:

> 'And you, of course, have perfect dress sense.'
>
> 'You poor thing, how do you manage to put up with having to eat out all the time? It must be hell for you.'

It's/Its see **Apostrophes**, page 53.

Judicial/judicious

Judicial means *to do with a court of law*.

> The judicial proceedings started this morning.

Judicious means *sensible.*

> John made a judicious decision when he agreed to sell his
> flat for £200,000.

⚠ **Watch out for *kind of* and *sort of***

Neither of these should ever be used to mean *somewhat.*
Use *fairly* or *rather* instead.

> He went home feeling kind of (rather) angry. His girlfriend
> had been sort of (fairly) miserable all evening and he
> didn't understand why.

Kind of and **Sort of** should only be used when referring to a
type of something.

> She brought some sort of cake with her but we couldn't
> decide what was in it.

Legend/myth

A legend is a *traditional story,* usually with some truth to it.

> The legend of King Arthur is based on a real English king.

A myth is *total fantasy.*

> A centaur is a creature of myth.

Libel/slander

Both are crimes involving making damaging statements, which
are proved to be untrue, about a person or persons.

Libel involves published material – it may be written in a book,
newspaper or magazine, or broadcast on television or radio.

Slander usually involves spoken words, but it can also take the form of gestures, signs and looks, such as pointing silently at an individual when a general accusation is being made.

Licence/license

Licence is a noun, meaning *certificate giving permission*. It may also mean the permission itself.

> You need a licence to own a television set.
>
> She was given full licence to spend as much money as she wished.

License is a verb, meaning *to certify*.

> It costs over £100 to license a television set.

Note that the difference between the two words is that the noun is spelt with a *c* and the verb is spelt with an *s*. Compare advice/advise, council/counsel, practice/practise, etc.

Lie/lay

To lie is intransitive.

> I lie down on the sofa.

To lay is transitive and needs an object noun.

> I lay the book down on the table.

Make sure you use the correct form in the past tense.

> Yesterday I lay down on the grass.
>
> Yesterday I laid the rug down on the grass.

Literary/literally

Literary means *of books.*

> My uncle was the literary critic for the local newspaper.

Literally means *using the primary sense of the word,* i.e. not figuratively.

> She was literally lifted off her feet by the wind.

The following are therefore complete nonsense.

> My feet were literally dropping off because I had run so far. ✗

> She was so happy she literally flew down the street. ✗

Using **literally** to intensify an exaggerated metaphor or simile is poor English:

> The twins were literally as alike as two peas. ✗

Loose/lose

You won't confuse the meanings of these two, but do make sure you get the spelling right.

> Her shoe was loose and it rubbed her heel.

> I hope I don't lose you in the crowd.

Luxuriant/luxurious

Luxuriant means *lush* or *prolific.* It can also mean *ornate* or *exuberant.*

> The rainforest was full of luxuriant vegetation.

> The luxuriant carvings on the ceiling were breathtaking.

> She had a luxuriant imagination which enlivened her conversation as she made up stories to entertain the children.

Luxurious means *full of luxury*.

> *The luxurious apartment had everything you could imagine for personal comfort.*

Masterful/masterly

Masterful means *exercising power* or *possessing authority* and is usually used to describe a person.

> *She loved the masterful way he always took charge.*

Masterly means *possessing and exercising skill* and is usually used to describe abilities or achievements.

> *The gymnast gave a masterly performance on the asymmetric bars.*

Meet/meet with

There is no need to add **with** when talking about meeting a person or thing.

> *I am going to meet my friend for coffee.*

Use **meet with** when talking about an incident.

> *I hope we don't meet with an accident on the motorway.*

⚠ **Watch out for *meet up* and *meet up with***

Don't use the phrases *meet up* or *meet up with*, they are incorrect. *Meet* is quite sufficient on its own.

> *We met up with some old friends last week.* ✗
> *We met some old friends last week.* ✓

Momentary/momentous

Momentary means *lasting only for a moment.*

> I had a momentary lapse of memory.

Momentous means *of great importance.*

> The meeting of the two presidents was a momentous occasion.

> ⚠ **Watch out for momentarily**
> Do not use **momentarily** to mean **after a moment.**
> > I'll be with you momentarily – just wait for me.   ✗
> It means **for a moment.**
> > She hesitated momentarily, then continued her speech. ✓

Moral/morale

Moral as an adjective means *concerned with ethical behaviour.*

> He had a moral obligation to look after his young sister when his parents died.

Moral as a noun means *a moral lesson.*

> The moral of the story was, 'don't let the grass grow under your feet'.

Morale means *mental attitude,* especially one of confidence.

> The morale of the team was high when they knew they had reached the final.

Nationalise/naturalise

To nationalise means *to take over on behalf of the state.*

> Many people think the railways should be taken out of private ownership and nationalised again.

To naturalise means *to admit (a foreigner) to full citizenship* or *to introduce (a plant or animal) into another habitat so that it flourishes in the wild.*

> My friend from Jamaica was naturalised last year and now has a British passport.
> Canadian mink that escaped from fur farms have now become naturalised in Britain.

Objective/subjective
Both adjectives are used to describe viewpoints.
Objective means *detached, unbiased.*

> He had researched all the evidence for and against the argument in order to give an objective view.

Subjective means *personal, emotionally involved.*

> As the father of the accused, his view of the crime was subjective.

Official/officious
Official means *authorised.*

> The Queen went on an official visit to Canada.

Officious means *bossy and interfering.*

> The doctor's receptionist was an officious woman who used her position to make life difficult for patients.

Orthopaedics/paediatrics/paedophiles
Orthopaedics is the branch of medicine dealing with the treatment of disorders of the bones and joints.

> The patient's arthritis was being treated by the orthopaedic surgeon.

Paediatrics is the branch of medicine dealing with the treatment of children and their diseases.

> The baby was admitted to the paediatric department.

Paedophiles are sexual deviants who display desire towards children.

Overtone/undertone

An overtone is a subtle meaning in addition to the main meaning.

> His apparently friendly smile had overtones of menace.

An undertone is an underlying *quality*.

> There is an undertone of sadness in all of Leonard Cohen's songs.

Pacific/specific

Pacific as an adjective means *characterised by peace, tranquil*.

> She gazed out into the deep, pacific darkness of the tropical night.
>
> The Pacific Ocean was so-named by the first sailors who rounded Cape Horn, because of its relative calm compared to the terrible storms they had encountered.

Specific means *precise*.

> The surgeon described in specific detail the operation I was about to undergo, so I would understand the procedures.

Peaceable/peaceful

Peaceable means *peace-loving*.

> They were glad the islanders were a peaceable community who offered them food and water.

Peaceful means *quiet*.

> I was glad when everyone else went out and I could have a peaceful evening by myself.

Perceptible/perceptive

Perceptible means *detectable*.

> There was a perceptible twitch of a smile on his otherwise stern face.

Perceptive means *insightful*.

> The perceptive GP knew that his patient's frequent headaches could not be entirely due to her recent illness.

Persecute/prosecute

To **persecute** means to *harass* or *discriminate against*.

> The Nazis persecuted the Jews.

To **prosecute** means *to bring to trial*.

> Trespassers will be prosecuted.

Personal/personnel

Personal is an adjective, meaning *belonging to oneself*.

> I put all my personal belongings in my handbag.

Personnel is a noun, meaning *staff* or *employees*.

> The memo said that all personnel must report to the manager.

Perspective/prospective

Perspective is a noun, meaning *a way of viewing things*, sometimes implying a sense of proportion.

> The jury must be given a clear perspective of all the circumstances surrounding the crime so that they can come to their verdict.

> Try to put all the events of the last few days into perspective – they are just an unfortunate series of coincidences, nothing to worry about.

Prospective as an adjective means *future*.

> My prospective partner is a high-powered executive.

Perverse/perverted

Perverse means *contrary* or *obstinately determined when in the wrong*.

> The perverse child demanded a biscuit and then wouldn't eat it.

> The alchemists persisted in the perverse belief that they could turn base metal into gold.

Perverted means *corrupt* or *deviant* (usually in a sexual context).

> The perverted man enjoyed watching pornographic films.

Possible/probable

A **possible** outcome is one that *can* happen.

> It is possible that I might win a prize in the raffle.

A **probable** outcome is one that *is most likely* to happen.

> It is probable that I won't win a prize in the raffle.

Practice/practise

Practice is a noun, meaning *a rehearsal, a custom* or *a professional group.*

> We have only one more practice before the concert tomorrow night.
>
> It is the accepted practice in some homes for people to remove their outdoor shoes before entering.
>
> There are two doctors in our village practice.

Practise is a verb, meaning *to do repeatedly, to carry out* or *to engage in (hobby or work).*

> I used to have to practise the piano for 30 minutes every evening.
>
> Practise what you preach.
>
> I have been practising yoga/medicine for over 30 years.

Precede/proceed

To precede means *to go before or in front of.*

> Spring precedes summer.

To proceed means *to go forward.*

> When crossing the road, it is safe to proceed when the road is clear.

Precedence/precedent

Precedence means *priority.*

> Sadly, earning money often has to take precedence over having fun.

A precedent means *a previous case or (legal) decision used as a guide for subsequent cases*.

> A precedent was set when the youth received a custodial sentence for slashing car tyres.

Precipitate/precipitous

To precipitate means *to bring forward in time, to cause to occur prematurely*.

> The shock of losing his wife precipitated the old man's death.

Precipitate as an adjective means *violently hurried*.

> The boys made a precipitate retreat when they came face to face with a bull in the field.

Precipitous means *dangerously steep*.

> Only the most experienced skiers attempted the precipitous slopes at the top of the mountain.

Presumptuous/presumptive

Presumptuous means *unduly confident*.

> The chairman's presumptuous behaviour made him very unpopular. The final straw came when he signed the agreement without even discussing it with the committee members.

Presumptive means *giving grounds for presuming that something is true*.

> The presumptive evidence of the boys' distinctive footprints in the ground outside the broken window was enough to convince the teacher to give them a detention.

Prognosis *see* **Diagnosis**

Prophecy/prophesy
Prophecy is a noun, meaning *a prediction of a future event.*
> *The prophecy that the world was going to end at the millennium turned out to be wrong.*

Prophesy is a verb, meaning *to foretell a future event.*
> *Estate agents prophesy continued growth in house prices for the foreseeable future.*

Provided/Providing *see* Verbs, page 14.

Quotation/quote
A quotation is a passage or line taken directly from a book, play or a repeated statement.
> *The quotation came from Shakespeare's play Macbeth.*

It may also be used to describe *an estimated price for a job.*
> *The builder gave us a quotation for replacing our windows.*

To quote means *to cite a passage or line from a book, play, etc.*
> *The priest quoted a passage from the Bible.*

It may also mean *to state a price for a job.*
> *The builder quoted £1000 to replace our windows.*

These days, the word *quote* is used colloquially to mean *a quotation*. Strictly speaking, this is incorrect and should be avoided.

Rebut/refute

Both verbs mean *to turn down an argument*.

To refute implies simply giving an indignant response, denying the argument.

To rebut has stronger overtones, implying that evidence is actually provided to counter the argument.

Recent/resent

You are unlikely to confuse the meaning here, but take care with the spelling.

> *We had a recent bereavement in the family.*
>
> *I resent having to pay such a high house insurance premium when I have never claimed for anything.*

Referee/umpire

Both **referee** and **umpire** refer to someone who enforces the rules and settles disputes in sports. Their usage depends on the sport involved.

> *Dicky Bird is probably the best-known umpire in English cricket.*
>
> *The referee blew his whistle to indicate the end of the football match.*

Referee may also be used to refer to *someone who testifies to the character of an applicant for a job, etc.*

> *I asked my boss if she would act as a referee for my new job application.*

Regal/royal
Regal means *fit for a monarch*.

> The Queen always behaves in a regal fashion.

Royal means *belonging to a monarch*.

> The royal procession included The Queen, Prince Philip and Prince Charles.
>
> The Queen Mother was probably the most popular member of the royal family.

Regretful/regrettable
Regretful is used to describe people, meaning *showing sorrow or regret*.

> She felt deeply regretful of her appalling behaviour at the party.

Regrettable is used to describe situations or actions and means *causing sorrow or regret*.

> I must apologise for my daughter's regrettable lack of decorum. I am told she behaved extremely rudely.

Repairable/reparable
Both these adjectives are to do with *making good*.

Repairable is used when referring to physical damage to objects.

> Fortunately, the broken chair was repairable.

Reparable is used when referring to loss, injury, etc.

> Fortunately the damage caused by his remarks was reparable and he was soon forgiven.

Regarding/as regards/with regard to

These are sometimes, but not always, interchangeable.

> *Regarding/As regards/With regard to your recent request for leave, I have to remind you that you have already used your full allocation for this year.*

Care should be taken with **regarding** at the beginning of a sentence, however. Remember that the subject of the main verb in the sentence must also be doing the regarding (*see* page 12).

> *Regarding the report, the statistics are misleading.* ✗

Generally, it is safest to use **with regard to,** but do not make the mistake of adding an *s*.

> *With regards to* ✗

Respectable/respectful

Respectable means *decent, highly regarded, deserving respect.*

> *He gained a very respectable mark in his final exams.*
> *Do try to look respectable for your interview.*

Respectful means *polite, showing respect.*

> *The chief mourners walked at a respectful distance behind the coffin.*

Restive/restless

Restive means *impatient, fidgety.*

> *The horses were restive, pawing the ground, impatient to be on their way.*

Restless means *unable to rest.*

> The storm made him so restless he could not lie still, let alone sleep.

Rigorous/vigorous

Rigorous means *very thorough.*

> I had to pass a rigorous medical examination before I was accepted into the air force.

Vigorous means *forceful, energetic.*

> The doctor has told me to take some vigorous exercise, such as dancing or running, every day.

Sceptical/septic

Sceptical means *inclined to doubt accepted opinions.* A person with such views is known as a **sceptic.**

> He took a very sceptical view of the traditional religious teachings, calling the ceremonies 'a load of mumbo-jumbo'.

Septic means *contaminated with bacteria.*

> With nothing to cover the wound on his arm, there was a danger that it would become septic.

> Our house was not on mains drainage. Instead, waste matter went into a septic tank, where it was broken down by bacterial activity.

Scotch/Scots/Scottish

Scotch means *pertaining to Scotland.* It is used of objects and should never be used to refer to the people of Scotland, as it is likely to cause offence.

> Scotch broth, Scotch eggs, Scotch whisky.

The Scots are the people of Scotland.

> The Scots have a fascinating history.

Scottish means *relating to Scotland or its inhabitants.*

> The Scottish Highlands are breathtakingly beautiful.
>
> He has a strong Scottish accent.

Seasonable/seasonal

Seasonable means *normal for that season/time of year.*

> The weather was seasonable for April – a mixture of sunshine and showers.

Seasonal means *relating to that season.*

> Carols are seasonal songs for Christmas.
>
> Serve with a selection of seasonal vegetables.

Sensual/sensuous

Sensual means *gratifying the senses.* It has strong sexual overtones.

> Eating chocolate is a truly sensual experience. Some women say they prefer it to sex!

Sensuous means *affecting or appealing to the senses.*

> She wore a heady, sensuous perfume.

Sewage/sewerage
Sewage is *waste matter.*

> There were no proper drains, and in summer the smell of
> sewage was overwhelming.

Sewerage is *the sewer system.*

> The plans for the new estate gave full details of the
> supporting infrastructure, including roads, schools, water
> supply and sewerage.

Shall/will *see* Verbs, page 15.

Should/would *see* Verbs, page 16.

Sociable/social
Sociable means *enjoying the company of others.*

> Our neighbours are very sociable. They are always giving
> parties.

Social means *relating to society* or *relations between people.*

> The social club in the village is where everyone meets on a
> Saturday night.
> She decided to join the social services as she wished to work
> with people.

Spasmodic/sporadic

Spasmodic means *occurring in fits and starts* or *caused by a spasm.*

The injured bird made spasmodic attempts to flap its wings.

Sporadic means *separate (in space or time)* or *occurring only here and there.*

Weeds grew up at sporadic intervals amongst the gravestones.

Stimulant/stimulus

Stimulant means *a substance that arouses or excites.*

Caffeine is a stimulant.

Stimulus means *something that motivates.*

Sunshine is the only stimulus I need to get out the barbecue.

Strategy/tactics

A strategy is an overall plan to achieve an objective.

She devised a strategy to improve the output of the factory.

Tactics are the individual parts of the plan that are carried out to achieve the objective.

In order to improve output, she implemented a variety of specific tactics, including employing extra workers and offering cash rewards for early completion of orders.

Substantial/substantive
Both adjectives mean the same, meaning *solid, stout, with considerable value* or *importance*.

Substantial tends to be used to describe people or things.

> Our neighbour won a substantial amount of money at the races last week.

Substantive tends to be used to describe situations or actions.

> The management and unions made substantive progress during their discussions on the new wages policy.

Testimonial/testimony
Testimonial means a *formal statement bearing witness to someone's character, qualifications or conduct*. It may also be used to mean some kind of tribute.

> The chairman read out a testimonial about my father's contribution to the firm during his 40 years there.
> The cricket team organised a testimonial match to raise money for their longest-serving player.

Testimony is the statement of evidence, usually legal.

> The woman's testimony was of great importance in the case.

That/which
These are both used to introduce *descriptive clauses*. They are often interchangeable.

> This is the road that leads to the park.
> This is the road which leads to the park.

Which may also be used to introduce a clause adding information that is separate from the main meaning of the sentence. In this case, it is preceded by a comma or a preposition, or enclosed between two commas. You cannot use **that** in this way.

> I usually take the road on the left, **which leads to the park**.
>
> The house **in which we lived for over 40 years** has been demolished.
>
> The door, **which was normally kept shut**, was standing wide open.

The meaning of a sentence may be altered by the way **which** and **that** are used. Look at the following examples.

> The dog, which had been only slightly injured, got up and ran away.
>
> The dog which/that had been only slightly injured got up and ran away. The other one died.

The first version concerns just one dog. We are told that it got up and ran away. In addition, we are told that it was slightly injured.

In the second version, we have to understand that there were two dogs. The first sentence identifies which dog got up, and then the final sentence explains what happened to the other.

Tortuous/torturous

Tortuous means *twisting and turning* or *convoluted*.

> We took a tortuous route down the mountain.

Torturous means *agonisingly painful*.

> Running the London Marathon was a torturous experience!

⚠ **Watch out for *try and***
Try and is widely used but ungrammatical.

He said he would try and arrive before ten o'clock. ✗

Try to is the correct version.

I will try to work harder in future. ✓

Urban/urbane

Urban means *of or in a city or town.*

We live in an urban area with a population of 10,000 people.

Urbane means *suave and refined.*

The handsome, urbane man was a real charmer with the women.

⚠ **Watch out for *town* and *city***
Towns are simply large urban areas.

City should, strictly speaking, be used only to describe large towns that have had city status conferred upon them by decree of government. This used to be by virtue of the fact that they contained a cathedral, but nowadays this is not necessary.

Use/utilise
To use is the more common expression, suitable in most cases.

> *I want to use my carpentry skills to make a cabinet for my mother.*

To utilise means *to put to (good) use.*

> *If I make the cabinet, I can utilise my carpentry skills.*

While/whilst
Both are correct.

Who/which
Both are relative pronouns.

Who should be used to refer to people. It may also be used for pet animals, since they are considered to be personalities!

Which is used for objects, events or collective nouns, like a flock of sheep.

> *The child, who had been following him through the streets, stole his wallet.*
>
> *Peter Pan's shadow, which seemed to have a life of its own, was shut in the cupboard.*
>
> *Smoky the cat, who was not afraid of dogs, turned round and spat at the puppy.*

Who/whom *see* Pronouns, page 29.

Chapter 5
Words that Sound the Same

The English language is renowned for having words that sound the same but are spelt differently and mean completely different things. These are called *homonyms*.

See also Confusing Words, page 84, and Tricky Spellings, page 198.

advice	noun	recommendation
advise	verb	to recommend
air	noun	atmosphere
heir	noun	successor
aisle	noun	passageway
isle	noun	island
I'll	verb	I will/shall
allowed	past participle of *to allow*	
aloud	adverb	out loud
altar	noun	table at a religious ceremony
alter	verb	to change

ate	past participle of *to eat*	
eight	noun	the number 8
aural	adjective	to do with the ear or hearing
oral	adjective	to do with the mouth or speech
bail	noun	financial guarantee bridge over cricket stumps
bail	verb	to secure the release of, by providing bail money to scoop water out
bale	noun	bundle (of hay, straw, etc.)
ball	noun	spherical object
bawl	verb	to cry loudly
bare	verb	to uncover
bare	adjective	naked
bear	noun	a heavy furred animal
bear	verb	to tolerate; to give birth to
bazaar	noun	market, (usually oriental)
bizarre	adjective	strange
beach	noun	sandy shoreline
beach	verb	to land on the shore
beech	noun	a type of tree
beech	adjective	made of beech wood

bell	noun	cup-shaped object that rings when struck
belle	noun	a beautiful woman
berth	noun	sleeping compartment ship's mooring place
berth	verb	to moor
birth	noun	beginning, arrival
blew	past participle of *to blow*	
blue	adjective	of the colour blue; sad
boar	noun	male pig
bore	noun	dull person tidal wave in estuary
bore	verb	to make weary by being dull to make a hole
bored	adjective	weary of something dull
board	noun	piece of wood
boarder	noun	lodger
border	noun	boundary
born	past participle of *to be born*	
borne	past participle of *to bear*	
bough	noun	branch of tree
bow	noun	a mark of courtesy
bow	verb	to incline the head or body as a mark of courtesy

boy	noun	male child
buoy	noun	floating marker
buy	verb	to purchase
by	preposition	beside, on, past
bye	noun	cricket run scored without the ball being hit
bye	abbreviation	goodbye
bridal	adjective	of, belonging to the bride
bridle	noun	harness, reins etc.
bridle	verb	to put on a bridle to curb to express resentment
broach	verb	to raise (a subject), make mention of
brooch	noun	piece of jewellery
callous	adjective	cruel, insensitive
callus	noun	hard skin
cannon	noun	a large gun
cannon	verb	to collide with
canon	noun	law (often of church) a member of the clergy a collection of books a musical composition
canvas	noun	coarse cloth
canvass	verb	to solicit votes

cast	noun	mould; group of actors
cast	verb	to throw
caste	noun	Hindu social class
ceiling	noun	upper interior surface of room
		upper limit (of wages)
sealing	present participle of *to seal*	
cellar	noun	basement store room
seller	noun	vendor
cereal	noun	grain crop
serial	noun	story etc. told in instalments
serial	adjective	sequential, forming a series
cheap	adjective	inexpensive
cheep	verb	to chirrup
check	noun	test of accuracy
		square pattern
		bill (US)
		receipt
check	verb	to make sure
		to examine
		to stop
cheque	noun	a written order to a bank
chord	noun	group of musical notes sounded together
cord	noun	string, flex, etc.

cite	verb	to name as an example
sight	noun	vision
		view
site	noun	position
site	verb	to place
coarse	adjective	rough
course	noun	route
course	verb	to flow
colonel	noun	army officer
kernel	noun	edible centre of a hard nut
complement	noun	full quota
complement	verb	to accompany, balance, make up a matching pair
compliment	noun	flattering remark
compliment	verb	to praise or flatter
confidant	noun	someone to share secrets with
confident	adjective	self-assured
		sure of success
core	noun	centre
corps	noun	group of people
council	noun	assembly
counsel	noun	advice
counsel	verb	to advise
councillor	noun	elected member of a council
counsellor	noun	one who gives professional guidance

crews	noun	groups of people (manning ships, etc.)
cruise	verb	to make a journey by sea
		to move at moderate speed
curb	noun	restraint
curb	verb	to hold in check
kerb	noun	stone edging to pavement
currant	noun	dried grape
current	noun	flow
current	adjective	of the present time
dear	adjective	beloved
		expensive
deer	noun	grazing animal
deceased	adjective	dead
diseased	adjective	infected
decent	adjective	respectable
		kind, obliging
descent	noun	downward slope
		the act of going down
dissent	noun	disagreement
dependant	noun	one who relies on someone else
dependent	adjective	needy
desert	verb	to abandon
deserts	noun	deserved reward/punishment
dessert(s)	noun	pudding(s)

device	noun	gadget
devise	verb	to invent
die	noun	one dice
die	verb	to expire
dye	noun	a colouring agent
dye	verb	to colour
disc	noun	a round, flat shape or object
disk	noun	a piece of computer equipment
discreet	adjective	diplomatic
discrete	adjective	separate
draft	noun	rough copy or outline
draught	noun	current of air
		a quantity of drink
		depth of water needed to float a ship
draw	verb	to sketch
drawer	noun	a storage compartment without a lid
drier (*also* **dryer**)	noun	machine for drying
drier	comparative adjective	more dry
dual	adjective	double, of two
duel	noun	a fight between two people

159

dyeing	present participle of to dye	
dying	present participle of to die	
eerie	adjective	weird, frightening
eyrie	noun	eagle's nest
elicit	verb	to draw out
illicit	adjective	illegal
ewe	noun	female sheep
you	personal pronoun	
yew	noun	a tree
faint	noun	a sudden loss of consciousness
faint	adjective	pale, indistinct slight, remote dizzy
faint	verb	to fall unconscious
feint	noun	pretence lines on paper sham attack
fair	noun	travelling show
fair	adjective	of light or pale colouring
fare	noun	tariff
farther	preposition	beyond
father	noun	male parent

faze	verb	to disconcert
phase	noun	a stage of development
phase	verb	to carry out in stages
feat	noun	noteworthy act
feet	noun	plural of foot
finish	verb	to end
Finnish	adjective	of the people of Finland
flair	noun	natural ability
flare	noun	a burst of flame
		a signal light
flare	verb	to burn
		to widen gradually
flea	noun	a type of insect
flee	verb	to run away from
flew	past participle of *to fly*	
flu	noun	influenza
flue	noun	chimney
flour	noun	grain that has been finely ground
flower	noun	a bloom
formally	adverb	officially
formerly	adverb	previously, in past times
foul	adjective	unclean
fowl	noun	poultry

freeze	verb	to chill
frieze	noun	wall painting
gait	noun	manner of walking
gate	noun	barrier
gamble	verb	to bet
gambol	verb	to frolic
gilt	noun	young sow
gilt	adjective	covered thinly with gold
guilt	noun	remorse
gorilla	noun	ape
guerrilla	noun	rebel
grate	noun	grid
grate	verb	to shred
great	adjective	big, grand
groan	verb	to moan
grown	past participle of *to grow*	
hail	noun	pellets of frozen rain
hail	verb	to pour down to greet
hale	adjective	strong, healthy
hair	noun	threadlike strands growing from skin
hare	noun	animal resembling a rabbit
	verb	to run very fast

hear	verb	to perceive (sound)
here	adverb	in, at, to this place
heard	past participle of *to hear*	
herd	noun	group of animals
him	personal pronoun	
hymn	noun	religious song
hoard	noun	stock, store, cache
	verb	to stockpile
horde	noun	crowd
hoarse	adjective	rough and croaking
horse	noun	a hoofed animal
hole	noun	cavity, empty space
whole	noun	total quantity
whole	adjective	entire
hold	verb	to grasp
		to contain
holed	past participle of *to hole*	
holy	adjective	sacred
wholly	adverb	completely
hour	noun	measurement of time, 60 minutes
our	possessive pronoun	belonging to us
are	verb	present tense of *to be*

key	noun	locking device
		solution
		musical pitch
quay	noun	dock, pier
knew	past participle of *to know*	
new	adjective	of recent origin, fresh
knight	noun	one awarded a hereditary title
night	noun	hours of darkness
knot	noun	fastening in a piece of string
		unit of nautical speed
		lump, node
not	adverb	expressing negation
lair	noun	den of an animal
layer	noun	a single thickness, coating
leak	noun	a hole that allows liquid etc. to escape
leak	verb	to seep out
leek	noun	a vegetable
licence	noun	certificate indicating permission
		the permission so accorded freedom
license	verb	to authorise, grant permission, issue a certificate

lightning	noun	flash of light during an electrical storm
lightening	present participle of *to lighten*	
loan	noun	a financial advance
loan	verb	to lend, make an advance
lone	adjective	single, by oneself
loath	adjective	unwilling
loathe	verb	to detest
loot	noun	plundered booty, stolen goods
loot	verb	to plunder
lute	noun	a musical instrument
made	past participle of *to make*	
maid	noun	female servant
mail	noun	items of postage, letters and parcels
mail	verb	to send by post
male	noun	a person/animal etc. of the male sex
male	adjective	masculine
main	noun	ocean domestic supply (of gas, electricity, etc.)
main	adjective	principal, greatest in importance
mane	noun	growth of long hair

meat	noun	flesh
meet	verb	to come together
meet	adjective	appropriate, suitable
medal	noun	a metal disc given as an award
meddle	verb	to interfere
meter	noun	gauge, mechanism for measuring
metre	noun	unit of measurement
mist	noun	haze, vapour
missed	past participle of *to miss*	
muscle	noun	sinew
mussel	noun	a mollusc
none	pronoun	not one
nun	noun	female member of a religious order
oar	noun	pole with a blade used to propel a boat
ore	noun	solid raw material from which metal or valuable minerals may be smelted
or	conjunction	(introducing an alternative)
oxen	noun	plural of ox
Oxon	abbreviation	Oxfordshire

pail	noun	bucket
pale	noun	stake for fencing
pale	verb	to fade, lose colour
pale	adjective	pallid, having little colour
pain	noun	ache, discomfort
pain	verb	to cause discomfort
pane	noun	sheet of glass
pair	noun	a couple, two
pare	verb	to peel
pear	noun	a fruit
palate	noun	roof of the mouth sense of taste
pallet	noun	portable wooden platform
palette	noun	board on which artist mixes colours range of colours
passed	past participle of *to pass*	
past	noun	times gone by
past	adverb	beyond
past	adjective	of a previous time
pause	noun	interval of silence, break
pause	verb	to stop momentarily, leave a break
paws	noun	plural of paw

peace	noun	calm
piece	noun	portion
peal	noun	ringing noise, series of notes (of bells)
peal	verb	to ring
peel	noun	rind
peel	verb	to remove the skin to come off in layers
pedal	noun	foot-operated lever
peddle	verb	to sell
peer	noun	lord of the realm an equal (in age, rank, etc.)
peer	verb	to look closely
pier	noun	jetty
place	noun	location
place	verb	to put in position
plaice	noun	a fish
plane	noun	aeroplane level surface imaginary line joining two points a type of tree tool for smoothing
plane	verb	to smooth to skim over
plain	noun	area of open land
plain	adjective	simple, unadorned

plum	noun	a stone fruit
plumb	adjective	perpendicular
plumb	adverb	exactly
poor	adjective	of low quality
		having little money
pore	noun	minute opening in a surface
pore	verb	to study closely, be absorbed in
pour	verb	to dispense liquid
		to fall heavily, flow
practice	noun	rehearsal
		custom
		professional work group
practise	verb	to rehearse
		to carry out, exercise
pray	verb	to implore
prey	noun	animal that is hunted and killed by another for food
prey (on)	verb	to hunt as prey, make a victim of
principal	adjective	main, most important
principle	noun	rule, fundamental truth as basis of argument
profit	noun	gain
profit	verb	to benefit (from)
prophet	noun	one who foretells events
		an interpreter of the Old Testament

program	noun	computer code
programme	noun	printed list of events
		television or radio broadcast
		syllabus
programme	verb	to encode
rain	noun	precipitation
rain	verb	to pour down
reign	noun	period during which
		someone rules
reign	verb	to rule
rein	noun	part of a harness
raise	verb	to lift
rays	noun	plural of ray
raze	verb	to destroy, tear down
rapt	adjective	engrossed in
wrapped	past participle of *to wrap*	
read	verb	to understand written
		symbols
reed	noun	firm-stemmed water plant
read	past participle of *to read*	
red	adjective	coloured red
real	adjective	genuine
reel	noun	spool
		a lively dance
reel	verb	to walk or run unsteadily

recover	verb	to get better
re-cover	verb	to cover again
right	adjective	correct
right	verb	to make correct
rite	noun	a ceremony or ritual
write	verb	to form symbols with a pen on paper
		to compose
ring	noun	circle
ring	verb	to call
		to peal (of bells)
		to encircle
wring	verb	to twist and squeeze
road	noun	route, way
rode	past participle of *to ride*	
rowed	past participle of *to row*	
role	noun	acting part in a play
roll	noun	bread bun
roll	verb	to move by turning
root	noun	origin
		part of a plant normally below ground
route	noun	way
route	verb	to direct

rose	noun	a flower
rose	past tense of *to rise*	
rows	noun	plural of row (a line)
rows	present tense of verb *to row*	
rye	noun	a cereal plant
wry	adjective	dry, cynical (humour) contorted, twisted (face, smile, etc.)
sail	verb	to travel by boat or on water
sail	noun	piece of material stretched over ship's rigging
sale	noun	act of selling, rapid disposal of goods at reduced prices
sauce	noun	liquid accompaniment to food impudence
source	noun	origin
source	verb	to check the origins of
scene	noun	setting
seen	past participle of *to see*	
scent	noun	perfume, aroma
sent	past participle of *to send*	
cent	noun	a unit of currency

sea	noun	ocean
see	verb	to observe
seam	noun	line of stitching
		layer (of rock etc.)
seem	verb	to appear
sew	verb	to stitch
sow	verb	to scatter seed
so	adverb	consequently
shear	verb	to shave, cut
sheer	adjective	steep
		almost transparent
		absolute (sheer good luck)
soar	verb	to fly high, rise above
sore	adjective	painful
sole	noun	flat fish
		base of foot or shoe
sole	adjective	only
soul	noun	spirit
son	noun	male offspring
sun	noun	star round which the earth orbits
stair	noun	one of a flight of steps
stare	noun	long look
stare	verb	to gaze

stake	noun	post
		sum of money bet on something
steak	noun	thick slice of meat
stationary	adjective	still, motionless
stationery	noun	writing materials
steal	verb	to take without permission
steel	noun	a metal
		an instrument for sharpening
steel	verb	to strengthen (one's resolve, etc.)
stile	noun	arrangement of steps to allow access over a wall
style	noun	manner
storey	noun	floor of a building
story	noun	tale
tail	noun	end, back
		hindmost part of an animal projecting behind the body
tale	noun	story
taught	past tense of *to teach*	
taut	adjective	tight

their	possessive pronoun	of or belonging to them
there	adverb	in or to that place
threw	past tense of *to throw*	
through	adverb	from beginning to end, between, among finished (Are you through?)
throne	noun	chair of State for sovereign or bishop
thrown	past participle of *to throw*	
thrown	adjective	unnerved, shaken
tide	noun	rise and fall of seas due to gravitational pull of the moon marked trend
tied	past tense of *to tie*	
time	noun	progress of events moment, occasion
time	verb	to measure the time taken
thyme	noun	a herb
to	preposition	for, towards
too	adverb	also
two	noun	the number 2

told	past tense of *to tell*	
tolled	past tense of *to toll*	
trooper	noun	soldier in the cavalry
trouper	noun	a travelling entertainer
vain	adjective	conceited
vane	noun	blade of a windmill
		instrument to show direction of wind
vein	noun	blood vessel
		a stripe of different colour (in cheese, marble, etc.)
		a fissure in rock
vale	noun	valley
veil	noun	thin material on headdress
veil	verb	to conceal
veracity	noun	honesty, truthfulness
voracity	noun	greed
waist	noun	the narrower middle part of a figure
waste	noun	refuse, unwanted material
waste	verb	to squander
waste	adjective	leftover, superfluous

wait	noun	pause, passage of time
wait	verb	to be expectant
		to defer action until
weight	noun	heaviness
		influence
		load
		block or disc of metal
waive	verb	to refrain from insisting on a right to
wave	noun	hand signal, usually of greeting
		long body of water that breaks on the shore
wave	verb	to signal with one's hand
		to give a curved form to
weak	adjective	feeble
week	noun	a period of seven days
weather	noun	climatic conditions
whether	conjunction	(offering a choice)
which	relative pronoun	
witch	noun	sorceress
		flat fish
who's	abbreviation	who is, who has
whose	possessive pronoun	of or belonging to whom

won	past tense of *to win*	
one	noun	the number 1
one	personal pronoun	
wood	noun	timber area of trees
would	conditional tense of *will*	
yoke	noun	wooden crosspiece of harness
yolk	noun	yellow part of an egg
your	possessive pronoun	of or belonging to you
you're	abbreviation	you are

Chapter 6
Beginnings and Endings of Words

Prefixes (beginnings) and suffixes (endings) modify the meaning of the basic word. It is important to use the right one or you can convey the wrong meaning. For instance, disinterested is not the same thing as uninterested.

See also Confusing Words, page 84.

Prefixes
These can be added to the front of words to change their meaning. The majority used to be joined to the base word by a hyphen but this is not necessary unless the meaning is ambiguous (*see* Hyphens, page 65). The following list contains some of the most common prefixes. Exceptions or special rules are indicated with some examples.

Prefix	Meaning	Example
a	on	ashore
a	not, without	amoral
		Use *an* if the word begins with a vowel, e.g. anarchy
ante	before	antecedent, antenatal

anti	against, opposite	*anticlimax, anticlockwise*
be	all around	*besmear, bejewelled*
bi	two or twice	*bigamy, bicycle*
by, bye	subordinate, secondary	*bystander, by-product, bye-laws*
circum	round	*circumnavigate*
co	joint	*co-author*
		Usually takes a hyphen
con	with	*conjoined*
contra	opposite	*contradict*
counter	retaliation, opposition	*counteract, counter-productive, counter-proposal*
de	down	*depress, descend*
	reversal	*de-ice, decentralise*
dis	not	*dissatisfied*
	separate	*disseminate, disembowel*
em	put into, make	*embroil, empower*
		This is a variation on the *en* prefix, used with words beginning with *b* or *p*
en	put into, make	*enslave, encourage*
ex	out of	*export*
ex-	former	*ex-wife*
for	giving up	*forswear*
	prohibition	*forbid*
fore	before	*forerunner, forecast*

il	not	*illegitimate, illegible*
		This is a variation on the *in* prefix, used with words beginning with *l*
im	not	*imbalance, immature, impure*
		This is a variation on the *in* prefix, used with words beginning with *b, m* or *p*
in	not	*incapable*
infra	below	*infrastructure*
inter	between	*international*
intra	within	*intranet, intravenous*
intro	between	*introduction*
ir	not	*irregular*
		This is a variation on the *in* prefix, used with words beginning with *r*
mis	wrongly	*misspell*
mono	single	*monologue*
multi	many	*multicoloured*
neo	new, revived	*neonatal, neoclassical*
non	not	*non-believer*
	nine	*nonagon*
para	adjacent or similar to	*paradox, paratyphoid*
per	through(out)	*perceptive, perennial*
pseudo	false, imitating	*pseudonym, pseudo-science*

post	after	postgraduate
pre	before	preliminary
pro	onwards, in front of	progress, prologue
re	again	retake
		Re takes a hyphen when the word begins with an *e* (re-examine) or when it is used in its compound form meaning something else, e.g. reform (improvement) or re-form (form again)
retro	back	retrospective
sub	under	submarine
super	over, above	superimpose, superintendent
sus	under	susceptible, suspend, sustain
		This is a variation on the *sub* prefix, used before *c, p* and *t*
trans	across, through	transatlantic, transparent
ultra	extremely	ultramodern
un	not	unknown
under	below, beneath	underground
vice	in place of	vice-chairman

⚠ **Watch out for doubling the last letter**
If the prefix ends with the same letter as the beginning of the word, you must leave both.
under + rate = underrate

Suffixes

These are added to the ends of words to change the meaning in a specific way. Some can be tacked on to the word without spelling changes but others follow the rules – and exceptions! – below. If this section looks a bit confusing and you only need to check a correct spelling or meaning (rather than understand how it works), just look up the word in Confusing Words on page 84, or Tricky Spellings on page 198. The list of suffixes I have included is by no means exhaustive but those I have not mentioned adhere to the same rules.

We have already covered some special suffixes, so they are not included here. These are the verb endings *-d* and *-ed*, which are explained on pages 16–17, and the comparative adjective endings *-er* and *-est*, which you will find on pages 32–33.

See also Changing Words from Singular to Plural, page 69.

Suffix	Meaning	Example
-able, -ible	being able to	suitable, reversible
-ability, -ibility	the ability to	suitability, reversibility
-al, -ate, -ative	of or relating to	musical, Italianate, argumentative
-ance, -ence	the specific quality of (noun)	resonance, decadence
-ant, -ent	of a specific quality (adjective)	resonant, decadent

-ant, -ent	person who produces an effect	*servant, president*
-arium	indicates a place	*planetarium*
-ation	the act of	*condemnation*
-dom	indicating power or control	*kingdom*
-er, -eer, -eur, -ier, -or	person carrying out an action	*player, mountaineer chauffeur, harrier, aviator*
-ess	female of the species	*lioness*
-ette	small	*cigarette,*
	imitation	*leatherette,*
	female	*usherette*
-ful	full of	*successful*
-ify	to make	*simplify*
-icle	little	*particle*
-ise, -ize	to make, become or treat as	*Americanise*
-ish, -ile	having qualities of	*girlish, infantile*
-ism	denoting an action, state, principle, etc.	*alcoholism*
-ist	someone who does or adheres to something	*florist, realist*
-ite	connected with	*Israelite*
-itis	inflammatory disease	*appendicitis*
-less	lacking, without	*needless*
-let, -ling	small	*droplet, duckling*
-ly	in the manner of	*quickly*

-ment	the state of being	devilment
-ness	the state or condition of	restlessness
-ock	small	bullock
-ous, -ious	full of	monotonous, gracious
-ship	number or group of, status	readership lordship

Rules for adding the endings

Suffixes beginning with a consonant

When the suffix begins with a consonant, you usually simply add it to the base word.

> free + dom = freedom
> fret + ful = fretful
> fear + less = fearless
> cut + let = cutlet
> prince + ling = princeling
> sad + ly = sadly
> puzzle + ment = puzzlement
> good + ness = goodness
> friend + ship = friendship

Exceptions to the rule

If a word ends with a consonant then *y*, change the *y* to *i* before adding the suffix.

> merry + ment = merriment
> happy + ness = happiness
> nasty + y = nastiness

If a word ends in *l* and you are adding *-ly*, double the *l* before adding the suffix.

> ideal + ly = ideally

Some words that end in *e* drop the final *e* before adding the suffix. These are exceptions that you just have to learn.

> ankle + let = anklet (also drops the *l*)
> argue + ment = argument
> awe + ful = awful
> due + ly = duly
> wise + dom = wisdom
> true + ly = truly
> whole + ly = wholly

Suffixes beginning with a vowel

When the suffix begins with a vowel, things become a bit more complicated. The basic working principles are listed here but if you find them hard to commit to memory, simply check through them when you are writing so that you can make sure you have everything correct. If you are interested in the infrastructure, you can consult a detailed grammar book.

There are three basic options.

Simply add the suffix
There are several types of word that remain unchanged when
you add a suffix.

Words of one syllable with a long vowel sound.

    priest + ess = priestess
    read + able = readable
    book + able = bookable

Words ending in a vowel then *w*, *x* or *y*.

    view + er = viewer
    vex + ation = vexation
    play + er = player

Words with two or more syllables with the stress on the first
syllable.

    differ + ence = difference
    element + al = elemental

⚠ Watch out for exceptions to the rule
In *kidnap, outfit, babysit* and *worship,* you double the final
consonant.

    kidnap + er = kidnapper
    outfit + er = outfitter
    babysit + er = babysitter
    worship + er = worshipper

If a word ends with two consonants after a short vowel sound.
> attend + ance = attendance
> convert + ible = convertible
> expect + ation = expectation

⚠ **Watch out for proper names**
Proper nouns do not follow any of the rules, so check!
> Glaswegian, Mancunian, Trotskyism

Double the final consonant before adding the suffix
There are two types in this group.

Words of one syllable that end with a short vowel followed by any consonant.
> stop + able = stoppable

Words with two syllables with the stress on the second syllable, except those that end with two consonants.
> be**gin** + er = be**gin**ner
> for**get** + able = for**get**table

Neither of these rules applies if the final consonant is *w, x* or *y* as these are never doubled in English spelling.
> pay + able = payable
> tax + able = taxable
> a**vow** + al = a**vow**al
> em**ploy** + able = em**ploy**able

> ⚠ **Watch out for exceptions to the rule**
> If the stress changes to the first syllable when the ending is
> added, do not double the consonant.
>   re**fer** + ence = **re**ference
>   con**fer** + ence = **con**ference

Drop the final e before adding the suffix
If a word ends in *e*, drop the *e* before you add the suffix.
    appreciate + ation = appreciation

> ⚠ **Watch out for exceptions to the rule**
> Keep the *e* if the word ends in a soft *c* or *g* before the *e*.
>   notice + able = noticeable
>   courage + ous = courageous

Is it -able or -ible?
As a general rule, use *-able* when base words end in *-ation*.
        determination, determinable
        irritation, irritable

Use *-able* after a hard *c* or *g*.
        duplicable
        navigable

If a word takes *-able*, it will also take *-ably* and *-ability*.
   suitable, suitably, suitability
   irritable, irritably, irritability

Use *-ible* when base words end in *-ion*.
   conduction, conductible
   diffusion, diffusible

Use *-ible* after a soft *c* or *g*.
   reducible
   illegible

If a word takes *-ible,* it will take *-ibly* and *ibility*.
   responsible, responsibly, responsibility
   possible, possibly, possibility

Is it -ance/-ant or -ence/-ent?
Use *-ance* and *-ant* when the companion word ends in *-ation*.
   variation, variance, variant

Use *-ance* and *-ant* after the sound of hard *c* or *g*.
   significance, significant

Use *-ant* for most words referring to people who do or are something.
   celebrant, sergeant, lieutenant, assistant

> ⚠ **Watch out for exceptions to the rule**
> There are exceptions, which you just have to memorise.
>   president, resident, superintendent

Use *-ence* and *-ent* after *-qu*.
    infrequence, infrequent

Use *-ence* and *-ent* after the sound of soft *c* or *g*.
    magnificence, magnificent
    negligence, negligent

Chapter 7
Abbreviations and Capital Letters

Abbreviations

Many abbreviations are used in everyday English instead of the full words. Here are the basic ones to do with language in general. It is sometimes difficult to know when to use them in written English. (*See also* Full Stops, page 57, and Capital Letters, page 194.)

c/o: Short for *care of,* this is used when addressing letters to persons for whom you do not have an address and so are sending their mail to the address of a third party who may forward it.

do: This is short for *ditto,* Latin for *already said.* It is used when you want to show that you are repeating something. This short form is often replaced with two commas (,,) underneath the word or number that is to be repeated.

e.g.: Short for the Latin expression *exempli gratia,* this means *for example* and should be used when you want to illustrate a point with one or more examples. This is **not** the same as *i.e.*

etc.: This is short for *et cetera,* Latin for *and other things.* It may be used when you wish to imply that a list may be extended to include more of the same or similar items. It is always preceded by a comma, but never the word *and (and etc.* is wrong), since this is already contained in the expression. In formal English it is better to write *such as* or *for example,* then list a few examples, rather than use etc.

ib or **ibid.:** This is short for *ibidem,* Latin for *in this place.* It is used mainly in reference books, to refer to something that has already been mentioned earlier.

i/c: Short for *in charge of,* this should not be used in formal writing.

i.e.: This is short for *id est,* Latin for *that is,* and is used when you want to clarify a point by saying it in another way.

inst.: Short for *instant,* this is used mainly in formal letters and documents, to mean *this month.*

NB: Short for *nota bene,* this Latin expression means *note well.* It is usually added at the end of a paragraph when you want underline the importance of something.

prox.: Short for *proximo,* this means *next month* in formal and business documents.

PS: Short for *post scriptum,* this means *written after* and is used to add an afterthought at the end of an informal letter. It should never be used in a formal letter. If you think of something you have missed, rewrite the whole letter.

RSVP: Short for the French *Répondez s'il vous plaît,* this means *please reply.* It should only be used at the bottom of an invitation and is usually followed by a deadline, an address and/or phone number or e-mail address. Do not use in a formal letter of any other kind.

sic: Usually in brackets, this is Latin for *thus* and is used where you wish to show that words quoted are reproduced exactly as they were spoken or written, despite what may appear to be mistakes.

ult.: Short for *ultimo,* this means *last month* and is used only in formal letters or documents.

Capital letters

Capital letters are not applied so rigidly today as they once were, but there are instances when they must be used.

To begin a sentence

All sentences must begin with a capital letter. It doesn't matter if there are no other capitals in the sentence. Allow a small space between the full stop of the previous sentence before starting a new one with its capital letter.

> Every sentence must begin with a capital letter. This is a simple rule of grammar. Unusually for English, there are no exceptions.

To begin direct speech
Open direct speech with a capital letter.

> The teacher said, 'Remember to use a capital letter when you start writing something in inverted commas.'

To begin proper nouns
Proper nouns – names, place names, titles, proprietary brands, etc. – always take a capital letter as do any adjectives derived from them.

> *The Oxford English Dictionary* is a useful reference book.
> My name is Carolyn Humphries.
> Paris is the capital city of France.
> She bought a packet of Quaker Oats.
> He tried to write his girlfriend a sonnet in Shakespearean style.

God obviously requires a capital letter, and some people always use capitals for words such as *He, His* and *Him* when referring to God. This is acceptable (although not in the case of *who* or *whom*), but it is not necessary and does not actually follow usage in the Bible or the Book of Common Prayer.

Compass points: Note that compass points as part of place names are proper nouns and so take capitals. When they are abbreviated to single letters, they must be capitals but when they are used as adjectives they do not take capital letters.

> We visited the West Indies and North Africa.

They go up to the West End every Saturday night.
The wise men came from the East.
Set the heading to NNE (north-north-east).
He travelled south for several days.
The west wind blew fresh in his face.

For special organisations

Capital letters should be used when a word is being used to refer to a specific organisation. Note the use of the same words, without a capital letter, as normal adjectives.

She joined the Conservative party.
His taste in jumpers is very conservative.
I belong to the Greek Orthodox church.
She had an orthodox, middle-class upbringing.

For many abbreviations

Many abbreviations and acronyms are written in capital letters. These may or may not need full stops (see page 57).

The EU (European Union) used to be the EC (European Community) and before that it was the EEC (European Economic Community)!
Learning your ABC is the first step towards becoming a good grammar student.

To begin lines of poetry, songs, etc.

Most traditional poetry starts each line with a capital letter, regardless of what punctuation (if any) there is at the end of the previous line. This extract is taken from Walter De La Mare's 'The Listeners'.

> 'Is there anybody there?' said the traveller,
> Knocking on the moonlit door;
> And his horse in the silence champ'd the grasses
> Of the forest's ferny floor:

To add impact

Whole words, or even whole sentences, may be written entirely in capital letters to convey excitement, volume, etc. This device should be used judiciously.

> BANG! The heavy, oak door slammed shut.

The pronoun I

This is always capitalised.

> I said that I would read the poem aloud.

Chapter 8
Tricky Spellings

Everyone has some words that they find hard to spell. This list covers those known to cause the most problems.

Remember the following rule:
> *i before e except after c*

It also helps to remember that
> *if it sounds like **a** – as in neigh*

the rule is **reversed**.

These ie/ei rules are true for most words but there are exceptions, **all** of which included in the list below, marked with an * to show they break the rule!

Where there are two acceptable spellings of a word, I have included both on the list.

See also Changing Words from Singular to Plural, page 69; Beginnings and Endings of Words, page 179; Confusing Words, page 84; and Words that Sound the Same, page 152.

A
abscess
abysmal
ache
acquainted
acquiesce
acquire
acreage
across
address
adviser
aesthetic
ajar
allege
aluminium
Alzheimer's
anaesthetic
analogue
anxiety
appal
apparatus
ascend
ascension
asphalt
assassin
asthma

audible
audience
authoritative
awkward

B
babyhood
bachelor
bazaar
beginner
bicycle
binoculars
bivouac
bizarre
boisterous
broccoli
building
bureaucracy
burglar
business
butcher

C
caffeine*
calendar
canister

captain
career
Caribbean
catarrh
catastrophe
categorical
cauliflower
chaos
cheque
chestnut
chimney
chronic
cigarette
clutch
colander
collapsible
colleague
college
colossal
comfortable
coming
commemorate
commission
committee
comparative
competitive

completely
computer
concede
connection
connoisseur
conscience
conscientious
consistent
contagious
contemporary
controller
convenience
convenient
correspond
counterfeit*
courageous
courteous
criticism
crystal
cupboard
curiosity

D
decrepit
deficient
definite

descend
describe
description
desiccated
destroy
deterrent
development
diaphragm
diarrhoea
dictionary
difference
difficult
dilapidated
dinghy
diphtheria
diphthong
disagree
disappear
disappearance
disappoint
disastrous
disciple
discipline
discrepancy
disease
disintegrate

dissatisfied
doubt
duchess

E
ecstasy
eczema
eighth
either*
eloquent
embarrass
encyclopaedia/
  encyclopedia
endeavour
enrol
enrolment
enthusiasm
environment
estuary
exaggerate
excellent
excite
exclamation
exercise
exhausted
exhibition

exhilarated
expendable
expense
experience
explanation
extraordinary
extravagance
exuberance

F
facetious
Fahrenheit*
familiar
fascinate
favourite
feasible
February
fiend
fiery
fifth
finish
flexible
fluorescent
forcible
forecast
foreign*

forest
forfeit*
forsake
fortunately
forty
frantically
frequent
fulfil
fungus

G
gaiety
gaily
garage
gauge
generous
ghastly
gipsy/gypsy
glamorous
gorgeous
government
graffiti
grammar
grandad/granddad
granddaughter
grandma

grandpa
grateful
grievance
grievous
guarantee
guardian
guest
guttural

H
haemorrhage
handkerchief
harass
headquarters
heifer*
height*
heinous*
hindrance
hippopotamus
hundred
hutch
hyena
hypocrisy
hypocrite

I

idiosyncrasy
immediately
immense
immoral
impossible
incidentally
indefensible
indelible
independence
indispensable
individual
inexhaustible
infectious
inflammable
information
ingenious
innocent
innuendo
inoculate
install
instalment
intelligence
intention
interesting
interrogate
interrupt
invisible
iridescent
irrational
irrelevant
irreparable
irreversible
itinerary

J

jealous
jeopardy
jewellery/
  jewelry
jodhpurs

K

keenness
khaki
knowledge

L

laboratory
landscape
language
legible
leisure*
liaise
liaison
library
lieutenant
  (pronounced
  'lef-tenant')
likeable
likelihood
liqueur
liquorice/
  licorice
literature
livelihood
lovable/loveable
luxury

M

machinery
mahogany
maintenance
manageable
manoeuvre
mantelpiece
margarine
marriage

marvel
marvellous
mathematics
meant
mediaeval/medieval
medicine
mediocre
Mediterranean
memento
mention
messenger
metaphor
meteorology
mileage
millipede
millennium
miniature
minuscule
miscellaneous
mischievous
moccasin
monastery
monotonous
mortgage
moustache
murmur

N
naïve/naive
necessary
necessity
neighbour
neither*
niece
ninth
nosey/nosy
noticeable
nucleus
nuisance

O
obedience
occasion
occurrence
often
omission
omit
ophthalmologist
opposite
original
outrageous
overreact

P
paediatrician
pageant
paraffin
paraphernalia
parliament
particle
particular
partner
passenger
pastime
peculiar
penicillin
people
perhaps
period
permanent
permissible
perpendicular
perseverance
phenomenon
physical
physique
Piccadilly
piccalilli
picnic

plateau
plausible
pleasant
pleasure
pneumonia
possess
possession
possibility
possible
prejudice
preparation
present
primitive
privilege
probable
probably
procedure
proclamation
profession
professor
profit
prominent
pronounceable
propaganda
protein*
psychiatrist

psychologist
publicly
pyjamas

Q

quarrel
quarrelsome
quarter
questionnaire
queue

R

radiator
raspberry
rateable
really
reasonable
recipe
recommend
refectory
refrigerator
register office
rehearsal
relevant
remember
renowned

repellent
repetition
representative
reservoir
resistance
responsibility
responsible
restaurant
restaurateur
resuscitate
reversible
rheumatism
rhyme
rhythm
ridiculous
rococo

S

sacrifice
sacrilege
salary
salmon
sanatorium
sandwich
satellite
Saturday

saucer
scarcely
scenery
sceptic
schedule
scheme
scholar
scissors
secretary
seize*
sentence
separate
sergeant
serviceable
several
severe
sheikh*
sheriff
shoe
silhouette
similar
sincerely
skilful
sovereign*
stimulant
stomach

subtle
subtlety
subtly
success
sufferance
suggest
supersede
surfeit*
surprise
surreptitious
survivor
syllabus
synchronise
synonymous
synopsis
syrup

T

tactics
tariff
technical
tee-shirt/ T-shirt
temperature
tendency
terrible
thorough

threshold
tolerant
tomorrow
tornado
traffic
tragedy
tragic
truly
twelfth

U

umbrella
unconscious
underrate
undoubtedly
unequivocally
unique
unmanageable
unmistakable
unnatural
until
unusual
useful

V

vegetable
vehicle
vengeance
ventilation
veranda/ verandah
veterinary
vice versa
vicious
vigorous
villain
violent
visible
visitor
vocabulary
voluntary
volunteer

W

watch
Wednesday
weir*
weird*
wharf
whether
whilst
wilful
wisdom
witch
woollen
wryly

X

X-ray
xylophone

Y

yacht
yoghourt/
    yoghurt/yogurt

Z

zealous
zoological
zoology

Chapter 9
Fancy Terminology

There are many techniques for jazzing up your English, to make plain ordinary speech into something a little more colourful and exciting. But of course, these forms of expression all have special names and if you don't know your similes from your metaphors, it's difficult to know where to start. In this chapter you will find a brief description of the most common terms and what they mean, together with examples of how to use them.

Acronym: A word made up of the initials of other words and pronounced as a word in its own right.

> AIDS (Acquired Immune Deficiency Syndrome)
> NATO (North Atlantic Treaty Organisation)
> CAT (Computer-assisted Testing)

Alliteration: Grouping together words that start with the same consonant. It may be used for some dramatic or poetic effect – but they are often used as tongue twisters!

> Cool, calm and collected
> Long, languid, lazy legs
> Peter Piper picked a peck of pickled pepper.

Analogy: Drawing a correspondence between two situations that are similar in certain respects. This is not the same as using a simile, where the comparison is more direct.

> *The arrival of the wet puppy in the drawing room had much the same effect as a stink-bomb.*

Anecdote: A short account of an interesting or funny incident.

> *My grandmother would take great delight in relating little anecdotes about my father and his many misdemeanours when he was young.*

Antonym: A word with the opposite meaning to another. These are usually presented in pairs, as you would expect.

> *hot and cold*
> *light and dark*

Cliché: A phrase that has been overused to the point where it loses any wit or descriptive merit it may once have had. Tabloid newspapers are a rich source of clichés, which should be...

> *... avoided like the plague!*

Colloquialism: An informal expression. This refers to everyday conversational style and does not mean slang. However, colloquialisms should be avoided in formal writing of any kind when you should try to use a more conventional turn of phrase.

We would love you to come over to us (visit us) this evening.
The boys prefer to hang out (spend their leisure time) without us these days.

Epigram: A short, pointed or witty saying.

A friend in power is a friend lost.

Eponym: A person after whom something is named, because they discovered or invented it. It has also come to mean the name itself.

sandwich (named after the Earl of Sandwich)
pasteurised milk (named after Louis Pasteur)

Etymology: The study of, or an account of, the sources of words and how their meanings have developed. Note that *entomology* is the study of insects; don't confuse the two!

On looking up the etymology of the word 'hydrophobia', I discovered that it comes from the Greek words for 'water' and 'fear'.

Euphemism: A vague or subtle expression used instead of a more direct, harsher one.

We lost my father last year. (My father died last year.)
She's somewhat vertically challenged. (She's very short.)

Homonym: A word that has the same sound but a different meaning from another – or several others. They may also have different spellings.

> Air and heir
> To, too and two

Hyperbole: An exaggeration, not meant to be taken literally.

> I have walked about a hundred miles on my ward rounds today.
> There were millions of people at the party.

Idiom: A figurative phrase that is understood because of long usage but bears no resemblance to the meaning of the words themselves. They are often peculiar to a country or language and so they don't translate well.

> taking the biscuit
> on a hiding to nothing
> keep your hair on

Litotes: An ironical understatement, usually negative.

> I shan't be sorry to see the back of him. (I'll be glad if he leaves permanently.)
> She's not exactly beautiful. (She's rather ugly.)

Malapropism: The substitution of a word for one that sounds similar – usually with amusing results.

Japanese pseudo-wrestlers are enormous!
I love watching Spanish flamingo dancing; it's so passionate.
She was always casting nasturtiums about people she disliked.
'I'm hopeless at grammar – all that punctuality and stuff!'

Metaphor: A figure of speech that applies an imaginative description literally to something.

Your face is the shining sun in my darkest night.

(This is not the same as a simile, which simply says that one thing is exactly like another. For example,

Your face shines like the sun.)

A metaphor can also suggest that something inanimate looks, behaves or sounds like something that is alive.

a glaring mistake
the cruel hand of fate
a biting wind

Metaphorical phrase: A phrase where the words that have a literal meaning are applied to mean something figuratively.

the tip of the iceberg (a hint of something much greater)
the cloud on the horizon (the disadvantage or drawback in something)

Mixed metaphors: Extending one metaphor can work well.

It will take the strong arm of the law to get a grip on the situation, collar those responsible and restore calm to our town.

However, linking two or more different ones can have extremely silly results.

> *The chairman decided to sit on the fence for the time being.*
> *He knew that if the wheels fell off the negotiations, his*
> *dreams would turn to dust, so there was no point in*
> *counting his chickens before they were hatched.*

Metonymy: Substituting another object for the object or person meant. They are readily recognised by most people and should not be taken literally.

> *The turf (horse-racing)*
> *The Crown (the reigning monarch)*
> *Downing Street (the prime minister)*

Onomatopoeia: Using words that make the sound that they wish to convey.

> *cuckoo, sizzle, miaow*

Proverb: A short, well-known saying that can be applied in a broader context.

> *A stitch in time saves nine. (It is best to try to take action early*
> *before a situation becomes worse and harder to remedy.)*

Rhetorical question: A question that doesn't expect an answer.

> *Do you want a smack?*
> *What are we going to do with you?*

Simile: A figure of speech that draws a direct comparison between two objects that are identical in some respect. Similes are usually preceded by *as* or *like*.

> as green as grass
> as dull as ditchwater
> scream like a banshee
> smile like an angel

Synonym: A word that has the same meaning as another.

> joy, pleasure and delight
> greed, voracity and gluttony

Syntax: Sentence structure. The simplest rules in English syntax are that adjectives go in front of the nouns they are describing; subjects go before verbs; and objects follow the verbs to which they refer.

See also Parts of Speech, page 7, and Sentences and Punctuation, page 43.

Tautology: Unnecessary repetition. This usually implies a fault since it involves saying the same thing twice.

> The children came into the room in succession, one after another.
> He accepted the invitation in the affirmative.

Usage Guide

Index